FROM ABACUS TO ZEUS
A HANDBOOK OF ART HISTORY

FROM ABACUS TO ZEUS
A HANDBOOK OF ART HISTORY

James Smith Pierce

Western Reserve University

PRENTICE-HALL, INC., *Englewood Cliffs, New Jersey*

Current printing (last digit): 10 9 8 7 6 5 4 3 2

Prentice-Hall International, Inc. [LONDON]   *Prentice-Hall of Australia, Pty. Ltd.* [SYDNEY]   *Prentice-Hall of Canada, Ltd.* [TORONTO]   *Prentice-Hall of India Private Ltd.* [NEW DELHI]   *Prentice-Hall of Japan, Inc.* [TOKYO]

PREFACE

ART must ultimately be explained in terms of art, not art terms. The description of visual form, the definition of stylistic categories, and the decoding of ancient myth and symbol, while fascinating pursuits in their own right, are of greatest value when they are mastered with the aim of comprehending the unique expressive power of individual works of art. This handbook has been prepared with that end in mind. Terminology and iconography have been defined with reference to specific works of art. This is done by keying entries to the splendid collection of over 900 reproductions in Professor H. W. Janson's phenomenally popular and accessible *History of Art.* Thus, terms, processes, principles, subjects, and symbols are not only defined verbally but can be studied as they appear in particular contexts and in historical sequence.

The "colorplates" which are referred to in the various entries are those in Janson's *History of Art;* numbers in italics (e.g., *271*) refer to Janson's figure numbers; and numbers preceded by "fig." refer to the drawings in this book. Words printed in *italics* are cross-references to other entries. If a term appears in italics, a definition of it will be found in alphabetical order in Chapter One; mythological beings will be found in Chapter Two; the subjects of Christian art, arranged by category, will be found in Chapter Three; saints, in Chapter Four; and Christian signs and symbols, in Chapter Five.

Simplified phonetic pronunciations are provided for unfamiliar names and terms, but they are only approximations of polite usage, introduced to prevent only the most ear-shattering barbarisms. In many cases, other pronunciations are equally acceptable. When a word has been taken over directly from a foreign language, it may usually be given the proper foreign pronunciation without raising too many eyebrows. Thus, "tablinum" (ta-bly'num) may even more "correctly" be pronounced ta-blee'num. In Chapter Four, the English names of saints are followed by their customary Italian, French, Spanish, and German names when the foreign form is markedly different from the English.

I am particularly indebted to Paulette Perone, who helped prepare the original list of entries, Arthur Irwin, who made many of the architectural drawings, Catherine Hartkopf, who typed the manuscript, H. W. Janson, who kindly consented to read the manuscript and gave me the benefit of his wise counsel, and all those students at Western Reserve University who insisted that I define my terms.

J. S. P.

CONTENTS

CHAPTER FIVE

MAPS

FROM ABACUS TO ZEUS
A HANDBOOK OF ART HISTORY

CHAPTER ONE

ART TERMS, PROCESSES, AND PRINCIPLES

ABACUS (ab′a-kus). The uppermost part of a *capital*, forming a slab upon which the *architrave* rests [*138*].

ABBEY (ab′ee). A *monastery* governed by an abbot. The church of an abbey is called an "abbey church" and is usually planned to allow for the special requirements of the monks such as a deep *choir* or many altars [*321–323, 329–331, 367, 368, 385, 386*].

ACANTHUS (uh-kan′thus). A prickly plant of the Mediterranean region with large, deeply cleft and scalloped leaves which are freely imitated on the *capitals* of the Corinthian and Composite *orders* and often used, in varying degrees of abstraction, to ornament *moldings*, brackets, *friezes*, etc. [figs. 26, 29, *149, 230, 275*].

ALTARPIECE. A painted or sculptured panel or shrine placed behind and above an altar, also called a "reredos" or "retable." Fourteenth- and fifteenth-century altarpieces are often very complicated, consisting of several panels or separate groups of sculpture. An altarpiece consisting of three panels is called a *triptych*; when it has more than three panels it is called a "polyptych" (pol-ip′tik) [*445–447*]. Some altarpieces have a decorated base, or *predella*, and have "shutters" or "wings" which can be opened in a series of "transformations" or "stages" to reveal other paintings or sculptures. The shutters are usually painted in rather subdued colors on the outside—monochrome imitations of sculpture ("grisailles") being common in Northern Europe [*447*]—but when opened up for the feast days of the Church, they offer a brilliant and sumptuous display of color [cf. *579* and colorplate 46].

AMBULATORY (am′byoo-la-toh-ree). **1.** A place for walking, usually covered, as the passage around a *cloister* or *peristyle*. **2.** The passageway around the *apse* of a church allowing circulation behind the high altar [fig. 10, *367*].

AMPHORA (am′fo-ra). A Greek storage jar with a large egg-shaped body and two handles, each springing from the shoulder of the jar and attached to the neck [*117, 119*].

ANDACHTSBILD (ahn′dahktz-bilt; pl. *Andachtsbilder*). Literally "devotional image," a term used for the highly emotive paintings and sculpture made, beginning in the late thirteenth century, for private devotion. Characteristic *Andachtsbilder* are such newly invented subjects as the *Pietà* [*408*] and "Christ as the Man of Sorrows," which emphasize personal grief and suffering.

APSE (aps, *not* ayps). A large niche facing the nave of a church. It is usually in the form of a half-cylinder covered with a half-dome [fig. 10, *254*, color-plate 13]; however, the apses of Byzantine churches, while semi-circular in plan on the interior, are often polygonal on the exterior [*268, 269, 273, 277*]. Many Byzantine and some Western churches are tri-apsidal, having two minor apses flanking the main apse [*277*]. Traditionally, the apse projects from only the eastern end of a church, but in some German churches there are apses at both east and west [*323, 330*]. Apses may also terminate the *transept* arms [*346, 347, 575*]. The many apse-like *chapels* projecting from the eastern flank of the transept arms and the *ambulatories* of Romanesque churches [fig. 10, *334*] are properly called "apsidioles."

ARCH. Almost any curved structural member which is used to span an opening is commonly, and very loosely, called an "arch" and the opening which it spans an "archway." In precise usage, however, the term is restricted to spanning members which are constructed of wedge-shaped blocks, called "voussoirs" (voo′swarz] [figs. 1, 5], which hold each other firmly in place

Fig. 1. Arcade.

and prevent each other from slipping because they are smaller at the bottom than at the top. An arch made of voussoirs is often called a "true arch" to distinguish it from structures which may have a similar shape (usually curved) but are constructed in some other way. A "corbeled arch," for example, is made of overlapping courses of stone, each block projecting slightly further over the opening than the block beneath it. The weight of blocks above the supported ends of the projecting blocks help prevent the unsupported ends from tipping and falling [fig. 2, *106, 107, 111*]. When

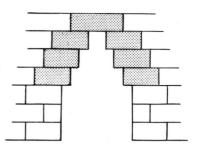

Fig. 2. Corbeled arch.

stone is used, a wider space can be spanned with a corbeled arch than with a single horizontal *lintel*, but the true arch is vastly superior to both in sturdiness and in the distances which can be spanned. The wedge-shaped voussoirs make full use of the strength of stone under compression while reducing the need for tensile strength to resist the bending and stretching caused by the pull of gravity or the downward pressure of a load above (*see* POST-AND-LINTEL CONSTRUCTION). The voussoirs at the top, or "crown," of the arch convert the downward pressure into lateral (sideways) pressure, or *thrust*, which is transmitted from the upper voussoirs down around the opening and finally into the ground through the wall or "pier" on which the arch rests [fig. 1]. Thus, the stones are relieved of the severe squeezing and stretching to which a lintel is subjected because of its tendency to sag where it is not supported. In a true arch, each voussoir supports its neighbor. The stones of a corbeled arch also support each other and are not subject to the bending pressures of a lintel, but they have unsupported ends which are subject to strong "sheering" stress, because the tip of each block projecting over the opening may be pinched off by the pressure of the blocks above, which press the tip against the edge of the block below. The true arch, however, is not without its own peculiar weakness. The lateral thrust is strongest at the "haunches" of the arch (the parts midway between the crown and the "springing") [fig. 1]. The "keystone," and the other voussoirs at the crown, press out against the voussoirs at the haunches, which may buckle and allow the crown to fall if they are not properly buttressed [fig. 3]. The lateral thrust at the haunches can be counteracted by the thrust of arches placed to either side, as in an arcade [fig. 1, *206*], but, unless the arcade is circular [*207, 208*], the lateral thrust of the arches at the end must finally be counteracted by the sheer mass of an "abutment" [fig. 1]. Many shapes and sizes of arches have been devised [fig. 4], but some are more efficient than others in overcoming the problem of lateral

Fig. 3. Failure of arch at haunches when keystone is driven downward due to overloading.

thrust. In general, it can be said that the more the shape of the arch approaches the vertical, as in the pointed arches used in Gothic construction [fig. 52, colorplate 21] and in some Romanesque churches [*336*], the more stable it will be. Conversely, the more closely it approaches the horizontal [fig. 4], the greater will be the lateral thrust and the weaker it will be.

Fig. 4. Various forms of arches (Sturgis).

Most arches do not spring directly from the ground but are raised on "piers" [fig. 1] or columns. When an arcade is supported on columns [*220, 253, 485*], it is sometimes called an "arcade-on-columns" to distinguish it from an arcade on piers [*206, 343*, 477], which is the more ancient and familiar type of arcade. After the foundation for the arcade is prepared, a "plinth" (base block) is usually laid for each pier. When each pier is finished, it is frequently capped with an "impost," upon which the lowest voussoirs, called the "springers," will be laid. The top of the impost, from which the arch will rise, or "spring," is called the "springing." Before the voussoirs can be set in place, however, a supporting frame, called the "centering," must be built. If the span to be arched is not

Fig. 5.

too wide, the centering can be placed on the impost and no additional support will be required [fig. 5]. The voussoirs are then laid up with mortar and, after the topmost voussoir, the "keystone," has been slipped into place, work must stop until the mortar has set. When the mortar is thoroughly dry, the centering can be taken down and used to construct another arch. The outside curve of the arch is called the 'extrados' and the inside curve is called the "intrados" [fig. 6]. The surface between any two arches of an arcade is called a "spandrel".

Fig. 6.

ARCHITECTURE. *See* ARCH, CANTILEVER, CHURCH ARCHITECTURE, DOME, ELEVATION, FERROCONCRETE, GREEK AND ROMAN TEMPLE ARCHITECTURE, MOLDING, MOSQUE ARCHITECTURE, ORDERS, PLAN, POST-AND-LINTEL CONSTRUCTION, PROGRAM, RUSTICATION, SCALE, SECTION, SKELETAL CONSTRUCTION, TRUSS, VAULT, WALL.

ARCHITRAVE (ar'kih-trayv). **1.** The lowest member of an *entablature*, resting directly on the *capitals* of *columns* or *pilasters* [fig. 29, *138*]. **2.** The *molding* framing a window or doorway [*151*, background; *226*].

ARCHIVOLT (ar'kih-volt). The *molding* framing an *arch* [fig. 1]. In Romanesque and Gothic architecture, each one of the series of arches framing the *tympanum* of a portal may be called an archivolt [fig. 45]; they are often highly ornamented or carved with figures [*338, 354, 396*].

ARTICULATED (ar-tik′yoo-lay-ted; fr. L. *articulare*, to divide into joints). Divided into distinct units; the term is often used in describing architectural designs [*335, 501*].

ASYMMETRICAL (ay-sih-met′rih-kul). Not symmetrical, but not necessarily unbalanced. *See* SYMMETRY, BALANCE.

ATMOSPHERIC PERSPECTIVE (also called "aerial perspective"). The representation of spatial effects which are caused by the interposition of the atmosphere between the viewer and distant objects; these effects include the blurring of outlines, loss of detail, alteration of *hue* toward blue, and diminution of color *saturation* and *value* contrast—all of these effects become increasingly evident with the distance of objects from the viewer. Atmospheric effects were represented by ancient Roman fresco painters [colorplate 9] and, after the long interval of the schematic art of the Middle Ages, again interested European artists beginning in the fourteenth and fifteenth centuries [colorplates 27, 35, 37, 40, 41, 46]. Chinese and Japanese painting during the period of the European Middle Ages was surprisingly atmospheric, although it was largely restricted to effects obtainable with black ink [*830, 835*]. Atmospheric effects, with the exception of shifts in hue and saturation, can also be obtained in *relief sculpture* [*165, 228–232, 475, 612, 662*].

ATRIUM (ay′tree-um). **1.** The open entrance court of a Roman house [fig. 19, *216*]. **2.** The open court in front of a church [*254, 343*].

ATTIC. A story above the main *entablature* of a classical building, frequently ornamented with *pilasters* aligned with the *order* below [*241, 546, 573, 598, 660, 677, 693*].

AXIS (*pl.* axes). An imaginary line passing through a figure, building, etc., about which its principal parts are arranged. In diagrams, the axis is usually represented by a broken line [fig. 7, *107, 295*].

BALANCE. The achievement of equilibrium among the various parts of a composition is a problem which all artists must face; indeed, for some artists, it appears to be among their most compelling concerns [*120, 154*, colorplates 53, 67, 72, 76, 77]. For the architect and sculptor it is more than a visual problem; it is a structural necessity as well, since every building or statue

Fig. 7. Vertical axis (a) of a figure from Masaccio's "Tribute Money."

must be physically supported in some way. By drawing analogies with such problems of purely physical balance, it is possible to suggest, in a limited way, some of the factors involved in visual balance. If the parts of a composition are represented as weights balanced on a seesaw, with the fulcrum standing for the vertical *axis* of the composition, it will be seen that one of the simplest ways to achieve balance is to place units of equal weight on either side of the fulcrum and equidistant from it [fig. 8a]. This is analogous to symmetrical composition in the visual arts [*134, 218*, colorplate 31, *492*]. Unequal weights may also be balanced by placing them at different distances from the fulcrum [fig. 8b, c]. This is analogous to asymmetrical, or "informal," balance [*7, 119, 332, 430, 499, 579, 586, 633*, colorplates 19, 67],

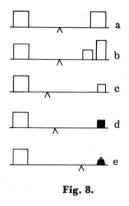

Fig. 8.

although, in pictures, objects of the same apparent visual "weight" appear to be heavier on the right-hand side of the picture than on the left. In the eighteenth century, such asymmetrical compositions in architecture, which were quite novel at the time, were called "irregular" [*686, 688*] to distinguish them from symmetrical, or "regular," buildings. There are many other factors, which are important in maintaining visual balance, that are less easily suggested by analogy to physical balance. Variations in *hue, value,* or *saturation* may alter pictorial balance by making one area more insistent than another. By darkening the little cube of fig. 8 c, for example, it is given apparent weight, because dark colors usually look heavier than light colors [fig. 8d]; yet, when the smaller cubes in both fig. 8c and fig. 8d are compared only to each other, the light cube looks larger than the dark cube, because lighter objects tend to look larger than darker objects. Altering the shape of the little cube can make it look even heavier, especially if that shape is associated with extremely heavy objects [fig. 8e]. This indicates that adjusting the parts of a composition may be much more than a formal problem. In representational art, associational or psychological factors must be taken into account. When a small area represents a face or a hand [*639*, colorplate 62], for example, it may have much greater psychological weight than a larger area which is not so highly charged with emotional interest. *See* SYMMETRY.

BALUSTRADE (bal'uh-strayd *or* bal-uh-strayd'). A handrail supported by short pillars, each called a "baluster" [bal'uster; fig. 40, *544*]. By extension, any low parapet [*318*]. On many Renaissance and Baroque buildings, balustrades appear above the main *entablature* [*530, 542, 545, 659, 660, 674, 684*].

BASILICA. Originally, any large hall, as the public halls erected by the ancient Romans on the fora, or public squares, of their towns [*205, 212–215*]. The term was adopted by the Early Christians to designate their churches which, since the new religion was congregational, were necessarily meeting-halls and retained some of the features of the familiar secular meeting-halls: colonnades, *clerestory* windows, and an "exedra," or *apse* [*253–255*, colorplate 13]. The term is sometimes applied to any church which, like the

Early Christian basilicas, has a longitudinal *nave* terminated by an apse and flanked by lower *side aisles*.

BAY. The space between any two of a series of similar architectural members, usually principal supports [fig. 10].

BLACK-FIGURED. A term applied to a type of Greek vase painting, practiced in the seventh and sixth centuries B.C., in which the figures and objects were painted primarily in black against a lighter ground, or field, usually the natural clay, which becomes orange-red after firing [*119, 120,* colorplate 5]. Details were crisply incised into the black figures before firing. *See* RED-FIGURED.

BLIND ARCADE. An arcade attached to a wall so that the arches, although they project from the wall, are not open but blocked with masonry [fig. 52, *336, 343, 345, 349*]. Any architectural features which are normally open, such as arches, windows, doorways, or *tracery* patterns, are called "blind" when their openings are blocked and they are simply used to ornament a surface [*378, 502, 542, 616*].

BLOCK BOOK. A type of devotional picture book, popular in the fifteenth century, in the production of which the text was carved in relief on the same block as the picture, rather than being set separately in movable type as became the practice later.

BOOK OF HOURS. A book for private devotions containing prayers for the different canonical hours of the day (matins, vespers, etc.). In the later Middle ages, books of hours were often sumptuously *illuminated* for the use of persons of high rank and, in addition to the various prayers, or offices, they frequently contained a calendar illustrated with the Labors of the Months [colorplate 25]. Books of hours are sometimes referred to simply as "Hours" and may be identified by the name of the owner, as the "Hours of Jeanne d'Evreux" [*438*] or *Les Très Riches Heures du Duc de Berry* ("The Very Rich Hours of the Duke of Berry") [*442*].

BURIN (byur'in). The pointed steel cutting tool, or graver, used to make the lines, or "tailles" (tai'ee; F.), of an *engraving* [fig. 9]. It is fitted with a broad wooden handle against which considerable pressure from the whole arm can be exerted through the palm of the hand to engrave the hard metal plate. The blade is grasped between the thumb and first or second finger.

Fig. 9.

BUTTRESS. A vertical mass of masonry built against a wall to strengthen it, often against the *thrust* of an arch or *vault* on the other side [fig. 10, *334, 339, 368, 371*]. The "flying buttress" system, used in Gothic churches, is a means of transmitting the thrust of the *nave* vaults through a masonry strut (often, itself, called the flying buttress) which carries it across the open space above the roofs of *side aisles* and *ambulatory* to a tall pier rising above the outer wall [fig. 52, *346, 372*].

CALLIGRAPHY (ka-lig'rafee; fr. Gk. *kallos*, beautiful, + *graphia*, writing). The art of ornamental penmanship or—in Chinese and Japanese writing especially—brushwork [colorplates 16, 79]. Drawings and paintings are said to be "calligraphic" (kalih-graf'ik) when they are essentially linear, resembling the spontaneous tapering and swelling of the cursive line and sudden accents of handwriting [*310, 326, 327, 792, 832,* colorplate 79].

CAMPANILE (kam-pa-nee'lee; fr. It. *campana*, bell). An Italian bell tower, especially one that is free-standing [*255, 343, 347, 389*].

CANTILEVER (kan'tih-leever). A beam or slab projecting a considerable distance beyond a post or wall but held down at one end only [*816, 817*]. By cantilevering structural steel beams and *ferroconcrete* slabs, twentieth-century architects have created overhanging stories which seem to defy the pull of gravity [*818, 823, 825*].

CAPITAL (fr. L. *capitellum*, little head). The crowning member of a *column*, *pilaster*, *pier*, or shaft. Column capitals, while forming a satisfying visual transition from the vertical shaft of the column to the horizontal *entablature*, may also increase the structural efficiency of the column by providing broader support for the load. Capitals are often richly ornamented, as the Egyptian papyrus capitals [*47*], the capitals of the Corinthian *order* [figs. 26, 29, *149*], or the Byzantine "basket capitals" [*270, 275*], but they may also be severely simple, as the capitals of the Doric order [fig. 29, *138–140, 144*] or the cubiform "cushion" capitals used in some Romanesque churches [*341*].

CARTOON (fr. It. *cartone*, a big sheet of paper). **1.** A humorous or satirical drawing [*723*]. **2.** A full-size drawing for a painting, made to be transferred to a wall, canvas, or panel as a guide in painting the finished work [*525*]. In *fresco* painting, the cartoon may be transferred by pricking it with a needle and "pouncing" it with charcoal dust so that the main lines of the composition appear as dots on the plaster surface of the wall.

CARYATID (karry-at'id). A female figure used as a column [*133, 150, 568*]. A male supporting figure is called an atlas (*pl.* atlantes; at-lan'tees); when the figure only partly emerges from a pedestal [colorplate 50, *603*], it is called a "herm" or "term" after similar figures of Hermes used to mark the terminal points of property in antiquity.

CASTING. A method of reproducing a work of sculpture by pouring a hardening liquid into a mold bearing its impression. In this way a piece of sculpture, created in a medium which is easily worked but perishable, can be preserved in one that is much more permanent. Bronze has traditionally been used for this purpose and for almost five thousand years it has been cast by the "cire-perdu" (seer per-doo'; F.), or "lost-wax" process. Because of the great weight and expense of bronze, solid casting is used for only very small figures; larger figures are hollow cast. In making a solid casting by the lost-wax process, the figure is first modeled in wax, allowance being made for the fact that the finished work will be in metal instead of translucent wax. The wax model is then surrounded with a mantle of clay. When the clay is dry, the whole piece is baked and all of the wax melted out through a hole. The molten bronze is then poured in to fill the hollows left behind by the wax. Before the cast can be removed, the mold too, must be destroyed. Thus, in the cire-perdu process, since neither the wax model nor the mold survive, only one cast can be made. To make a hollow casting, a core of clay is made first and the wax is modeled over it. When the piece is finished, it is covered with a mantle of clay, as in solid casting, and the wax is melted out. Metal rods, inserted through the mantle and core, hold them firmly in place during the melting process. The narrow space, which is left between them, is then filled by the molten bronze. When the mantle is broken and the core removed, the hollow shell of the bronze cast remains. A large piece of sculpture must be cast in several separate sections which can later be riveted or welded together. After the bronze has hardened, it is "chased" with hammers, chisels, files, and gravers to remove imperfections and to bring out or add details. Since a complex system of channels and ducts must be made in the mold to allow for the escape of wax, for the pouring of bronze, and for the escape of air as the bronze is poured, chasing involves the removal of the several projections which are usually formed by excess bronze flowing into these channels during casting. After chasing, the cast may be treated with acids to form the surface coloring—usually greenish—called "patina" (pa-tee'na; It.), which may also be produced naturally through outdoor exposure, burial, or immersion in water for long periods of time.

When more than one cast is desired, the sand casting method may be used. In this process, the plaster model [*735, 753*], which may itself have been cast from a clay or wax original, is tightly packed in firm, damp sand mixed with loam. When half of the sand mold has been made, the iron frame which holds it is turned over together with the model and the other half of the mold is made. The model is then removed and, if the cast is to be hollow, a sand core is made by packing sand into the mold, after treating it to prevent the core from sticking to it. Once the core has been formed, it is removed from the mold and its surface is shaved so that a space, as wide as the desired thickness of the cast, is left between the core and the mold. Then, as in the lost-wax process, the core is suspended within the mold by rods driven through them both; the channels for the introduction of the molten bronze and for the escape of the air are cut; the mold is dried in an oven; its surfaces are smoked to prevent the metal from sticking; and finally the bronze is poured. After the bronze has cooled, the mold and core are removed and the cast is chased. Since the model has not been destroyed, as in the lost-wax method, an "edition" of many casts can be made by simply repeating the process.

CATHEDRAL. The church of a bishop, containing his "cathedra" or throne.

CELLA (sel'la; L.). **1.** The main chamber of a Greek or Roman temple, built to house the cult image [*137*]. **2.** The whole main body of a temple, excluding the *portico*.

CHAPEL. 1. A small church [*319, 486, 538*]. **2.** A compartment in a church containing an altar dedicated to one of the many saints, but often referred to by the name of the donor [*611*]. The chapels projecting from the *ambulatories* of Romanesque and Gothic churches are called "radiating chapels" [fig. 10; *367, 368*].

CHARTREUSE (shar-trurs'). A *monastery* of the Carthusian order [*409*].

Fig. 10. Plan of S. Sernin, Toulouse.

(a) nave.
(b) side aisle.
(c) transept.
(d) crossing.
(e) choir.
(f) apse.
(g) ambulatory.
(h) chapels
    (apsidioles).
(i) buttresses.
(j) bay.

CHÂTEAU (sha-toh'; *pl.* châteaux; sha-toh' *or* sha-tohz). The French word for castle, applied originally only to fortified dwellings, but now, to any French country house [colorplate 25, *596, 629*].

CHIAROSCURO (kyah'ro-skoo'ro; It. fr. *chiaro*, light, + *oscuro*, dark). The gradations of light and dark within a picture, especially one in which the forms are largely determined, not by sharp outlines, but by the meeting of lighter and darker areas [*522, 564, 635–642*]. *See* VALUE, TONE, SFUMATO.

CHOIR. The area in a church reserved for singers and clergy, usually extending from the *crossing* to the *apse*; also called the "chancel" [fig. 10]. Sometimes, as in "pilgrimage choir," the term denotes the entire east end of a church beyond the crossing, including apse, *ambulatory*, and radiating *chapels* [*368*]. This larger unit may also be called the "chevet" (sheh-vay'; F.).

CHOIR SCREEN. A screen, often elaborately carved, separating the *choir* from the *nave* of a church [*405*]. In England, the choir screen is called a "rood screen," because it is usually surmounted by a cross, or "rood" [*341*]. In Byzantine churches, the choir screen, decorated with *icons*, is called an "iconostasis" [*278*].

CHURCH ARCHITECTURE. *See* ALTARPIECE, AMBULATORY, APSE, ARCHIVOLT, ATRIUM, BASILICA, BAY, BLIND ARCADE, BUTTRESS, CAMPANILE, CATHEDRAL, CHAPEL, CHOIR, CHOIR SCREEN, CLERESTORY, CLOISTER, COMPOUND PIER, CROSSING, CRYPT, DOME, DRUM, GABLE, HALLENKIRCHE, LANTERN, MOSAIC, NARTHEX, NAVE, PENDENTIVE, PINNACLE, QUATREFOIL, RESPOND, RIB, ROSE WINDOW, SACRISTY, SARCOPHAGUS, SIDE AISLE, TRACERY, TRANSEPT, TRIFORIUM, TRUMEAU, TYMPANUM, VAULT, WEST WORK.

CLERESTORY (or Clearstory). A clear story, i.e. a row of windows in the upper part of a wall [fig. 52, *213*]. In churches, the clerestory windows above the roofs of the *side aisles* permit direct illumination of the *nave* [*255*, colorplates 13, 21, *336, 369, 374*].

CLOISTER (kloys'ter). **1.** A court bounded by covered walks or *ambulatories*, frequently found on the south side of the churches of monasteries [fig. 28]. **2.** The covered walk of such a court, usually provided with an *arcade* or colonnade.

CODEX (*pl.* codices, ko'dih-seez). A manuscript in the form of the type of bound book used today. The codex replaced the scroll, or "rotulus," of antiquity.

COFFER. **1.** A casket or box. **2.** A recessed panel in a ceiling [*211, 485, 492, 550, 615, 690*]. A coffered ceiling appears to be massive, but the coffering may actually make it lighter.

COLLAGE (ko-lahj'; fr. F. *coller*, to glue). A composition made by pasting various materials, such as strips of newspaper, wallpaper, cloth, etc., to a flat surface [*781*].

COLOR. *See* HUE, VALUE, SATURATION, PRIMARY COLOR, SECONDARY COLOR,

COMPLEMENTARY COLOR, COOL COLOR, WARM COLOR, SHADE, TINT, FLAT COLOR.

COLOSSAL ORDER. Any *order* in which the *columns* or *pilasters* rise through more than one story [*503, 545, 546, 574, 607, 677*].

COLUMN (kol'um). A cylindrical upright or *pillar*. All columns of the classical *orders*, except the Greek Doric, consist of a base, a tapered shaft, and a *capital* [fig. 29]; the Greek Doric column has no base [*131*]. Columns are usually used in a row (colonnade), with a space (intercolumniation) between each column, to carry an *entablature*, an arcade, or other load, but they are also sometimes used singly for decorative or commemorative purposes [*233, 622*]. "Engaged columns" are columns which, instead of being free-standing, are attached to a wall; they may be "half columns" or "three-quarter columns," which cast a deeper shadow than half-columns [*47, 151, 200, 208, 502, 574–577, 607, 616, 619, 674*]. Although engaged columns are essentially non-structural, they serve to *articulate* the wall and to express visually the support which the wall actually provides. Columns which are placed slightly in advance of a wall, but which carry projecting sections of the entablature, are said to be "en ressaut" [en (nasal) ressoh, F.; *213, 219, 241*].

COMPLEMENTARY COLOR. A *hue* which complements another in that they form a neutral gray when mixed together, but present a sharp contrast when juxtaposed. Contrast increases with the *saturation* of the two hues, highly saturated complementaries appearing to vibrate or flicker when set side by side. The complementary of any one of the *primary colors* is obtained by mixing the other two primaries: the complementary of red is green (yellow + blue), the complementary of yellow is violet (red + blue), and the complementary of blue is orange (red + yellow). The colors represented in the "color wheel" in fig. 11 are ar-ranged so that they are directly opposite

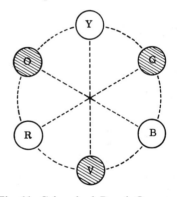

Fig. 11. Color wheel. R, red; O, orange; Y, yellow; G, green; B, blue; V, violet.

their complementaries. Complementary contrasts have long been used in works of art to intensify the effect of the color composition [colorplates 1, 10, 14, 62, 74], but complementaries were first used as part of a scientific program by Seurat and other "pointillists." The pointillists went so far as to imitate the effect of the projection of "negative after-images" onto the visual field outside the eye [colorplate 67]. Negative after-images are the patches of complementary color formed in the retina by prolonged exposure of the eye to colors of high saturation.

COMPOSITION. The organization or arrangement of the forms in a work of art. In making and evaluating works of art, organization is of such central importance that many works are simply titled "Arrangement" or "Composi-

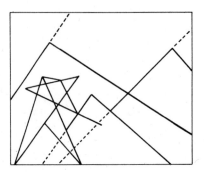

Fig. 12. Schematization of angular shapes on the picture plane.

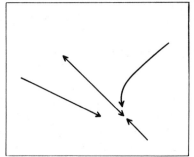

Fig. 13. Major movements across the picture plane.

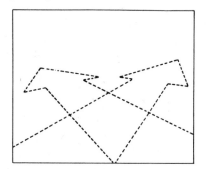

Fig. 14. Movements back into the picture space.

Fig. 15. Forward movement through the picture space.

tion" [*745*, colorplates 74, 76]. Some of the individual concepts and principles of composition which are commonly used are discussed under separate entries (*see* ATMOSPHERIC PERSPECTIVE, AXIS, BALANCE, CHIAROSCURO, COLOR, CONTOUR, CONTRAPPOSTO, DRAPERY, FIGURE-GROUND RELATIONSHIP, FOCAL POINT, FORESHORTENING, FRONTAL, GROUND-LINE, GROUND PLANE, LINE, MODELING, MOTIF, PERSPECTIVE, PICTURE SPACE, PICTURESQUE, PLAN, PLANE, PROFILE, PROPORTION, RHYTHM, SCALE, SHADOW, SHAPE, SUBJECT, SYMMETRY, VANISHING POINT, VIEWPOINT, VOLUME). Here, however, their interrelation within a single work is considered in a brief analysis of Rembrandt's "The Blinding of Samson" [*635*]. One of the very great pleasures in looking at this work, or any work of art, is the discovery of different patterns and relations among the forms and colors. These patterns are often so intermixed and superimposed that there can be no single prescribed way of distinguishing them; the observer will select different patterns at different times according to his "mental set" at the moment and he will relate them differently to the expressive content of the work. In a sense, then, there are many pictures within any single picture; it is rarely possible to single out only one pattern as *the* composition. Some of the larger patterns that can be distinguished in "The Blinding of Samson" are diagramed in figs. 12–17. These crude diagrams are worthless in themselves; they do not provide the "key" to the work,

Fig. 16. Curving and interlacing forms.   **Fig. 17.** Pattern of lights and darks.

but are meaningful only in so far as they bring out, by contrast with their crudity, the unique subtlety of variation within the broad patterns they describe. Fig. 12 indicates the sharp angular shapes that, within the context of the subject, are very aggressive. Their edges form a set of dynamic oblique relationships that are anchored only by the horizontal and vertical edges of the canvas. The only vertical in the picture is the rigid arm of the soldier who holds Samson firmly to the ground. Fig. 13 indicates the major directional lines on the *picture plane* which point with excruciating concentration to the gouging of Samson's eye. Only the major oblique *axis*, running from the upper left-hand corner to the lower right, can be interpreted as also pointing decisively away from Samson, because the fleeing figure of Delilah —who holds the hair and scissors which have cost Samson his strength—is disposed along this axis. One naturally looks back and forth between the cause (the hair) and the effect (the gouging). Fig. 14 indicates the two major movements back into the *picture space*. The figures have been disposed along these two crossing paths and receive something of their great energy from the dramatic rushing movement. The figure of the halberdier, in the extreme foreground, provides a shallow secondary thrust into the picture space as he points his weapon at Samson's face. The spatial movement might also be interpreted as in fig. 15, rushing forward along the line of soldiers, turning at Samson's head, and then rushing off again in the opposite direction back along the hurtling body of the fleeing Delilah. Fig. 16 indicates the complex pattern of interlacing forms which tells both on the picture surface and in depth, activating the larger compositional movements in a tight knotted rhythm that adds to the tension of Samson's moment of anguish. The twisting and turning is tightest toward his bound body and is almost inseparable from his own contorted limbs. Fig. 17 indicates the broken and twisted pattern formed by contrasting areas of light and dark which also contributes to the movement and tension of the scene. The areas of greatest emotional impact—Delilah's face, the scissors, Samson's head—are spotlighted; *highlights* glinting from the armor and weapons of the soldiers offer a hard contrast to Samson's vulnerable flesh. The red costume of the halberdier, Delilah's blue-green skirt and Samson's yellow trousers also contrast sharply and mark the conflicting parties, but effects of *hue* and *saturation*, while usually essential to the composition of a painting, can only adequately be studied in the original. The most accurate diagram of the color composition or the finest color reproduction is no substitute. A diagram lacks the sensuous appeal and delicate modulations of the original; the reduced size and imperfect color of a reproduction will always upset the balance of compositional elements to some degree. The full impact of all the formal elements working together can only be received while one stands before the original. Everything which one has studied about art is a preparation for that experience. It is a contemplative experience which takes a great deal of time and even something of the creative power of the artist who made the work, because, in many respects, looking at works of art is a *recreative* activity: one must select and analyze the formal elements and consider their expressive force much as the artist himself did while putting them together.

COMPOUND PIER. A *pier* with *columns, pilasters,* or shafts attached to it, frequently used along the *naves* of Romanesque and Gothic churches [fig. 52, *336, 341, 342, 344, 373, 381, 384, 391*]. The attached members usually support or respond to arches or *ribs* above them.

CONNOISSEUR (kon-ih-sur'; F.). A person—often a museum curator, art collector, or art dealer—who is devoted to the study of individual works of art and the personal *styles* of individual artists. Connoisseurs are particularly concerned with gauging the quality and condition of works with respect to others of their kind and to distinguishing among originals, copies, replicas (copies by the same artist who made the original), and outright forgeries.

CONTINUOUS NARRATION. The representation, within a continuous spatial setting, of events which occurred at different times, so that the same characters may appear more than once. This may be done by spreading out the individual episodes along a continuous band, similar to the arrangement of a comic strip but without divisions between episodes [*233,* colorplates 10, 38, *262, 362, 425, 440, 498*], or the different episodes may be arranged in depth so that earlier events appear in the background [*452, 477, 493*]. In the course of the sixteenth century, continuous narration was largely abandoned in favor of unity of time and place.

CONTOUR. The outline of an object or *shape,* especially when it suggests *volume* or mass. In "contour drawings," in which the outlines of objects are set down with little or no *modeling,* it is possible to suggest their roundness and solidity with a force that is surprising when one considers the extreme simplicity and abstraction of the technique [*15, 166, 198, 244, 310, 327, 770, 832*]. One of the ways in which this is done is by breaking or blurring the contour lines to suggest the disappearance of a surface as it curves out of sight. If the different contour lines touch each other too frequently, they may create two-dimensional shapes which tend to flatten the figure. Another way to enhance the apparent *plasticity* of the forms is by varying the thickness of the lines to bring some parts forward and others back; a sudden accent or swelling indicates the fullness of the form and a tapering line suggests its attenuation.

CONTRAPPOSTO (kon-tra-pah'stoh; It. fr. L. *contrapositus,* placed opposite). The graceful disposition of the parts of the body so that they turn along oblique axes arranged around a central vertical *axis* as in a figure looking back over his shoulder while striding forward [*167, 180, 250, 604*]. In extreme forms, the head, torso, legs, and arms may be twisted to such an extent that they are turned in nearly opposite directions and almost literally "counterposed" [*169, 182, 183, 525, 668*]. Usually, however, they are simply "counterpoised," attention being paid to "ponderation" (the distribution of weight throughout the figure) so that the weight-bearing leg, or *engaged leg*, for example, is distinguished from the raised leg, or *free leg*, and the resulting shift in the axes of hips and shoulders is observed. Above all, the stiff *frontality*, parallel alignments, and rectangular contrasts of direction, which are characteristic of Egyptian and Archaic Greek sculpture, are avoided [cf. *51, 52, 99, 124, 125*]. Contrapposto was developed by Greek sculptors and painters as a means of avoiding such stiffness and increasing the animation of their figures [*153–183*]. During the sixteenth century, the device was pressed to extremes of virtuosity and was often pursued for its own sake as a formal exercise or as proof of artistic skill, the problem being to make the members of the body elegantly conform to an imaginary three-dimensional spiral running continuously through the entire figure [*559, 568–570*].

COOL COLORS. Blue and associated *hues* such as blue-green and blue-violet. Cool colors normally appear to recede and *warm colors* to project.

CORNICE (kor'nis). **1.** The topmost member of a classical *entablature* [fig. 29, *138*]. **2.** Any horizontal member projecting from the top of a wall [*491, 810*].

CRENELLATED (kren'eh-layted; fr. Old Fr. *crenel*, a notch). Furnished with battlements, i.e. notched parapets placed at the top of a fortified building [*86, 394*, colorplates 23, 25, *433, 686*]. Each indentation in a crenellation is called a "crenel" and each solid section, a "merlon."

CROMLECH (krahm'lek). A prehistoric monument formed of great stones set on end and arranged in a circle, as at Stonehenge [*22, 23*].

CROSSING. The area in a church where the *transept* intersects the *nave* [fig.10], sometimes covered with a *dome* [*347, 682*] or marked by a "crossing tower" [*334, 379*].

CRYPT (kript). A *vaulted* chamber, wholly or partly underground. In a church, the crypt, housing a *chapel* or tomb, is usually located under the *choir*, which is, as a result, sometimes raised considerably above the level of the *nave* [*330, 331, 344*].

DIPTYCH (dip'tik). Two panels or leaves hinged so that they can be folded together. In late antiquity small ivory diptychs were carved with delicate reliefs for commemorative and religious purposes [*265, 266, 480*]. In the later Middle Ages, diptychs for private devotional use were painted with an image of Christ or the Virgin on one panel and the owner—sometimes recommended by his patron saint—on the facing panel [*458*].

DOLMEN. A prehistoric monument composed of huge upright boulders (megaliths) supporting a massive slab in such a way as to form a chamber, generally thought to have served as a tomb [*21*].

DOME. A *vault* of regular curvature raised on a circular or polygonal base. The pressures at work within a dome are similar to those within an *arch*. Thus, if one imagines the shape of a circular dome to be formed by rotating an arch around its vertical *axis*, it will be understood that there will be

considerable *thrust* at the haunch, as in
an arch [fig. 3], as well as around the
base of the dome. To counteract this
thrust, the dome may be loaded at the
haunch, as in the Pantheon at Rome
where a stepped abutment is used [*210*;
cf. *617*]. This, however, diminishes the
exterior effect of the dome. To increase
the visibility of the dome, it may be
raised on a cylindrical or polygonal
drum [fig. 18, *277*, *529*, *681*], but a
dome of any size, when it is removed
from the body of the building and lifted
high in the air, may have to be held
together with chains or rings of heavy

Fig. 18. Dome: (a) pendentive, (b)
drum, (c) dome, (d) lantern.

timbers to counteract the outward thrust. The height and curvature of a
dome may also be enhanced by covering it with a lighter and more prominent outer dome [*280, 389, 546, 663, 675*]. *See* LANTERN, PENDENTIVE.

DOMUS (doh′mus). The Latin word for "house." A large house of a well-
to-do Roman family and its servants, such as those excavated at Pompeii
[fig. 19, *216*], consisted of groups of rooms clustered around two open courts:

Fig. 19. (Mau).

the *atrium*, which was semi-public in that it was used for receiving guests
and conducting business, and the *peristyle*, a private garden surrounded by a
colonnade. Before entering the house, which was built close to the street,
one stepped into a recess (vestibulum) between the street and the door and,
after entering, walked through a short passage (fauces) to reach the atrium
which had a shallow pool (impluvium) in the center to catch the rain drop-
ping through an opening in the roof. Walking through the atrium, one passed
deep recesses (alae, or "wings"), to either side, and might then enter the
ambulatory around the peristyle either by going through the wide recess
called the *tablinum* or through a narrow passage (andron), to one side of it,
which could be used when the tablinum was occupied. A broad and deep
recess (exedra), corresponding to the tablinum of the atrium, was often placed
at the rear of the peristyle.

DONJON (dun′jun; F.; archaic English spelling of 'dungeon'). The *keep* or
central tower in a castle.

DRAPERY. The draping of fabric is one of the most important expressive devices available to the sculptor or figure painter, often exceeding in importance the posture and gesture of the figure which it clothes. Sometimes drapery dominates most of the visible surface of a work and requires only a hint of an associational context to convey almost by itself, through abstract form, most of the expressive content of the work [227, 354, 397, 469, 590, 648]. Drapery was developed by the Greek sculptors as a graceful linear counterpoint to the full volumes of the body; toward the end of the fifth century B.C., the blending of flesh and fabric in figures clothed with "wet drapery" became a prime artistic problem [162, 164, 165]. "Flying drapery" was introduced to enhance the apparent movement and excitement of figures [163, 167, 169, 181] and remained an important expressive device throughout the Middle Ages [332, 355, 363, 429, 461] and long after [472, 475, 500, 513, 604, colorplates 36, 46, 62, 69, 732, 802]. During the sixteenth century, wet drapery was again treated as a formal problem in very much the same way as it had been in antiquity [colorplate 43, 599]. When placed in an appropriate context, drapery can be charged with a broad range of emotional qualities from the most forbidding stillness [271] or profound gravity [170, 476, 585], through flights of gaiety [colorplate 57] and frivolity [678], to the heights of religious exaltation and ecstasy [562, 610]. The power of drapery as a vehicle of expression explains, in large measure, the use of flowing garments in portraits, even after close-fitting clothes had become the fashion [728, 730, 753].

DRÔLERIES (droh-leh-ree); F. fanciful designs of a playful character in the margins of medieval manuscripts [438] or on church furniture such as choir stalls.

DRUM. A cylindrical or polygonal wall rising above the body of a building, usually introduced to support a *dome* [fig. 18, 269, 270, 277, 389, 528, 529, 546, 663, 681, 682].

DRYPOINT. A print made from a design scratched into a metal plate with a steel needle held like a pencil [468]. In drypoint, which is really a form of *engraving*, the curl of metal, or "burr," turned up at one or both sides of the furrows which are scratched into the metal, is not scraped away as it is in regular line engraving, but is often left on the plate to hold thick deposits of ink [fig. 20b]. In printing, which is carried out in the same way as in engraving, the burr leaves deep velvety blurs of ink that are particularly effective in creating rich atmospheric effects. Drypoint is often used in conjunction with engraving and *etching*; Rembrandt, in particular, used it to deepen the *chiaroscuro* of his etchings [640].

ECHINUS (eh-kai′nus). In the Greek Doric *order*, the quarter-round (ovolo) *molding* beneath the *abacus* [138].

ELEVATION. 1. One side, or face, of a building. 2. An undistorted and measurable drawing of one side, or part of a side, of a building [131, 168, 194, 691]. To avoid *foreshortening* or convergence of parallel edges, the building is presented parallel to the *picture plane*.

ENAMEL. Colored glass applied to metal in powder or paste form and fused by firing. In the Middle Ages, two basic types of enamelling were used, "cloisonné" and "champlevé." In making cloisonné (klwah-zoh-nay'; F. fr. *cloisonner*, to partition) enamels [*313*], the surface to be decorated is divided into compartments with strips of metal ("cloisons"), usually gold; the compartments are then filled with enamel and the whole piece fired in a kiln. In making champlevé (shah [nasal] -luh-vay'; F. fr. *champ*, field, + *lever*, to raise) enamels, the areas to be filled with enamel are dug out with a cutting tool. Often, broad areas of metal are left raised and decorated by engraving. The engraved lines are usually filled with a black substance called "niello" (nyel'lo; It.) to make them more clearly visible [*365*]. The extraordinary transparency and translucence of enamels satisfied the medieval taste for glowing color [cf. colorplates 14, 18–21].

ENCAUSTIC. (en-kaws'tik; fr. Gk. *en*, in, + *kaiein*, to burn). A method of painting with molten wax much practiced in antiquity [colorplate 11, *287*]. Although encaustic colors are remarkably brilliant and durable, the technique has never been widely revived.

ENGAGED LEG. The leg on which a standing figure appears to place its weight. *See* FREE LEG, CONTRAPPOSTO.

ENGRAVING. A print made from a design cut with a *burin*, or graver, into a metal plate. Engraving is an intaglio (in-tal'yo) process rather than a relief process like *woodcut*, i.e. lines are cut into the surface of the plate and it is these lines that are printed, whereas, in making a woodcut, the spaces between the lines of the design are cut away, leaving the lines raised in relief [fig. 20a]. Engraving, then, is a "positive" process; the lines, or "tailles" (tai-ee; F.), made by the engraver with his burin are directly registered in the print. Lines are not easily cut into the metal plate (usually copper), so to facilitate cutting, the plate is often placed firmly on a small cushion filled with sand. The burin is held in one hand and, as it is pushed forward, the other hand is used to rotate the plate against the pressure of the burin. Thus, engraved lines are normally curved; they are thin where the burin begins the cut, they swell as more pressure is applied, and they taper again as the burin is lifted from the plate [fig. 21a, *467*, *583*, *584*]. After cutting, the plate is burnished to remove the bits of metal (burr) still clinging to the sides of the tailles [fig. 20b]. Ink is forced into the engraved lines with a dabber or roller, but ink remaining on the surface is entirely wiped away unless special tonal effects are desired.

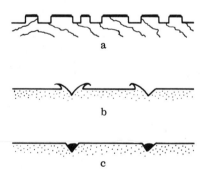

Fig. 20. (a) Cross-section of woodcut with lines inked. (b) Cross-section of engraved plate with double "burr" and single "burr." (c) Cross-section of engraved plate with "burr" burnished away, lines inked, and surface wiped.

If this is the case, smudges of ink may be left on the surface of the plate. The paper that is to receive the impression is dampened to ease its entry into the ink-filled furrows under the very great pressure of the press; the forcing of the paper into the furrows accounts for the characteristically raised lines of intaglio prints. The plate, with the paper placed on top of it, is passed on a heavy metal plate, or "bed," between two steel rollers arranged something like the clothes-wringer on a washing machine. The pressure of the rollers forces the whole plate to dig into the paper, leaving a distinct

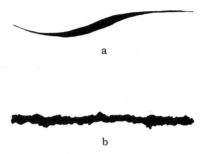

Fig. 21. Exaggeration of the characteristics of (a) an engraved and (b) an etched line.

"plate mark" around the edges of the print; this clearly distinguishes intaglio prints from woodcuts and *lithographs* which are not subjected to such great pressure. As in most printmaking processes, the printed design is reversed, a fact which must be taken into account while cutting the plate. Since the more delicate lines of the plate are soon damaged by the pressure of the rollers, engravings are usually issued in limited "editions." Since the nineteenth century, it has become customary to indicate in pencil on the margin of each print its precise number in the sequence of impressions; thus, the inscription '23/50' would indicate that the impression is the twenty-third in an edition of fifty. After taking the specified number of impressions, the plate should be "canceled." This is sometimes done by engraving a large 'X' across it and sometimes the plate is simply polished smooth and used to make another engraving. Sometimes the plate will be reworked after an edition has been "pulled" and a new edition of the plate will be printed; in this case, the different editions are distinguished as "State I," "State II," etc. Trial impressions taken in the course of cutting are called "proofs."

ENTABLATURE (en-tab'la-chur). The group of horizontal members resting on the *columns* or *pilasters* of one of the classical *orders*. The entablature is usually divided into three major parts: *architrave, frieze,* and *cornice* [fig. 29, *138, 144, 150, 151, 201, 256, 492, 545*]. Sometimes the entablature may break forward from the surface of the wall and project over columns and pilasters [*219, 241, 502,* colorplate 58, *674*] and sometimes it may be used, without supporting members, to terminate the top of a wall [*681, 682, 684, 689*].

ENTASIS (en'ta-sis). The gently swelling convex curvature along the line of taper of classical *columns*. The entasis of columns gives them a sense of elasticity as though they were responding to the load of the *entablature* above them. Moreover, entasis prevents the sense of weakness that results from the illusion of concavity in straight or regularly tapered columns. The entasis of early Greek Doric columns [*140*] is pronounced, but becomes ever more subtle until, in the columns of the Parthenon [*143*], it is barely perceptible.

ETCHING. A print made from a design scratched with a needle into an acid-resistant coating, or "ground," covering a metal plate and etched, or "bitten," into the metal by immersion in acid [*640, 716*]. The acid will only attack the parts of the metal (traditionally copper) which have been exposed by scratching away the ground. The longer the plate is left in the acid bath, the deeper and wider will be the lines etched into the metal and the darker they will appear when printed. Repeated bitings may be made to develop certain areas while others are "stopped out" with varnish to prevent further biting. When the artist is ready to make a trial impression, or "proof," the ground and stopping-out varnish are removed with a solvent and the plate is printed in the same way as an *engraving*, since both are intaglio processes. If the etcher wishes to eliminate some lines, he may scrape them out; if he wants to deepen some lines or add others, he may reground the plate and proceed as before or simply reinforce lines or add others by engraving with a *burin* or scratching with a *drypoint* needle. Etched lines appear much coarser and freer than engraved lines and unless the etcher intentionally imitates engraving, they will not have the even, curving, swelling and tapering character typical of engraved lines [fig. 21]. Since etching is a much less demanding and more flexible technique than engraving, it largely replaced it as a medium for creative artists during the sixteenth century. Steel engraving, however, long remained a standard medium for book illustration, because a much larger number of impressions can be taken before the lines begin to break [*617*].

FAÇADE (fa-sahd'). The front or principal face of a building, but, sometimes, any one of its sides [*338, 371, 392, 395, 501–503, 545, 577, 675, 693*].

FERROCONCRETE (or Reinforced Concrete). Concrete strengthened with steel rods and mesh which are laid up within the formwork before the concrete is poured. The steel adds tensile strength to the usual strength of ordinary concrete under compression. Introduced in France during the nineteenth century, it is now more widely used for large buildings than masonry or steel frame construction. A great variety of textures and patterns can be created by leaving the rough imprint of the formwork in the surface of the concrete [*825–828*]. Other variable factors within the control of the architect are the choice of color and the composition of the aggregate with which the cement is mixed. The variety of forms and shapes into which the concrete and the reinforcing rods can be set is practically infinite.

FÊTE GALANTE (fayt ga-lahnt'; *pl.* fêtes galantes; F., elegant fete or entertainment). A term used to describe the subjects of many of the paintings of Watteau and his followers in which elegant young men gracefully and rather wistfully court fashionably dressed young women in parklike settings [colorplate 55, *669*].

FIGURE-GROUND RELATIONSHIP. The relation of any object, shape, or line to the "field," or background, against which it is seen. The "figure," which is seen as a positive element, always appears to lie in front of the continuous "ground" running behind it. Even the black letters on this page seem to lie slightly in front of the white ground of the paper. Every time a figure is isolated as an object of interest it appears to lie against a ground. In some cases, however, the relation may be so tenuous that a reversal of figure and ground may occur; this frequently happens in abstract designs in which the area occupied by the ground is nearly equal to that filled by the figure. The wave motif on the plinth of the column base shown in fig. 27, for example, can be seen either as white waves against a dark ground or dark waves against a light ground. The desire to separate figure from ground is so strong that it is very difficult to see both the white waves and the black waves as lying together in the same plane. An artist is usually careful to avoid any ambiguity between figure and ground and makes his figures stand out by establishing a clear contrast with their grounds. Sometimes, the "negative shapes," formed by the parts of the ground lying between the outlines of the figures, can be used to support and reinforce the character of the "positive shapes" of the figures. This is particularly true when both positive and negative shapes occupy about the same area and have a similar configuration when isolated as figures by themselves [*103, 167*, colorplate 8, *169, 761, 764*].

FINIAL (fin'ee-ul; fr. L., *finis*, end). A terminal ornament at the highest point of a *gable, pinnacle*, spire, gate-pier, etc. [fig. 52].

FLAT COLOR. In painting, any color that is broadly applied with little or no *modeling* or variation of texture, *hue, value,* or *saturation* [colorplates 8, 12, 17, 72, 75–77]. When used in representational painting, flat colors normally indicate the "local color," or basic hue, of an object: green for grass, blue for sky, brown for wood, etc.

FLUTING (floot'ing). The decorative treatment of the shaft of a *column, pilaster*, or other surface with shallow, vertical grooves (flutes). In the Greek Doric *order*, adjacent flutes form a sharp edge, or "arris" [*144*], but in the Ionic, Corinthian, and Composite orders, they are separated by a flat surface called a "fillet" [fig. 29, *149*]. The fluting on the lowest third of a shaft is sometimes filled with a convex *molding* to protect the fillets, in which case the flutes are said to be "cabled" [*487, 492, 503, 509, 612, 624*, colorplate 58].

FOCAL POINT. In any composition, representational or abstract, a dominant area of major interest upon which the eyes focus more frequently than on others. If a picture contains a *vanishing point* it may or may not be a major focal point [cf. *524* and *559*]. Some compositions forming a continuous all-over pattern may have accents but no major focal points at all [*297, 792, 798, 824*].

FORESHORTENING. A method of representing objects or parts of objects as if they were seen at an angle and receding into space instead of being seen in a strictly *frontal* or *profile* view. The rod drawn in fig. 22a is shown in an unforeshortened side view, but the rod in fig. 22b is represented as though it were seen obliquely and appears to project or recede. The effect is achieved by employing the principle of continuous diminution in size along the entire

Fig. 22. Rod: (a) unforeshortened, (b) foreshortened.

length of the receding object. The term is reserved for single objects only and is not applied to regular diminution used in suggesting the recession of a large interior space or landscape. In the eighteenth and nineteenth centuries, when a critic praised an artist's "drawing," he generally meant his skill in handling difficult problems of foreshortening (*603, 654, 718*). *See* PERSPECTIVE.

FREE LEG. The lifted leg of a standing figure. Unlike the *engaged leg*, it bears little weight. *See* CONTRAPPOSTO.

FRESCO (It., fresh). A painting made on fresh, wet plaster with *pigments* suspended in water [*245–250*, colorplates 9, 10, 32, 58, *433–436, 492–494, 603–605*]. The fresco technique is usually used for decorating walls and ceilings. The plaster absorbs the colors and, when it dries, makes a very durable painting that is literally part of the wall, not simply applied to its surface. Since plaster dries rather quickly, only a small section, large enough to be painted at one time, is laid up with wet plaster. In Italian fourteenth-century frescoes, this final layer was usually applied over an outline drawing (*sinopia*) of the composition, which had previously been made on a layer of rough plaster. Since the artist must work quickly, completing the part to be painted before the plaster dries, the medium encourages a rather broad technique which reveals the individual brushstrokes [colorplate 38]. The colors in true fresco painting are much paler than those in *oil painting* or *tempera* painting, because they are absorbed by the white plaster. True fresco painting is sometimes called "buon fresco" (boo-on fres'ko; It., good fresco) to distinguish it from "fresco secco" (fres'ko sek'ko; It., dry fresco), the method of painting on the surface of the dry plaster with pigments mixed in a binding medium—a much less permanent technique which often results in flaking [colorplate 22]. In practice, both techniques were usually employed: "buon fresco" for the basic painting and "fresco secco" for touching up. Fresco painting was especially favored in Italy from the time of the ancient Romans through the eighteenth century.

FRIEZE (freez). **1.** The middle member of an *entablature*, between the *architrave* and the *cornice* [fig. 29, *138*]. In the Doric *order*, the frieze is decorated with *triglyphs* and *metopes* [*143, 146, 529, 684, 685*] and in the other orders it may be carved with various ornaments, figures, or inscriptions [fig. 26, *133, 151, 201, 210, 218, 503, 509, 577, 598*], but it may also be left bare [*200, 617*, colorplate 58, *545*]. **2.** Any long horizontal band of ornament resembling a frieze, whether decorated or not [*178, 180, 226, 228, 242*, colorplate 10].

FRONTAL. An adjective used to describe an object which faces the viewer directly and is not set at an angle or *foreshortened*. A "frontal view" is one in which the viewer places himself directly opposite one of the principal faces of an object. In early stages of the development of the arts, frontal and *profile* views are usually favored over "angle views" [*52*, colorplate 2, *54, 124, 129, 350, 397, 423*]; in later stages of development, angle views may be favored over frontal and profile views [*4, 177, 183, 243, 249, 377, 409, 559, 569, 813, 814*]. *See* VIEWPOINT.

GABLE (gay'bul). **1.** The triangular area formed by the slopes of a pitched roof at the end of a building; it extends from the eaves or *cornice* to the ridge of the roof [*255, 329, 376*]. In classical architecture, the gable is called a *pediment*, **2.** Any member resembling a gable in shape, such as the triangular structures erected over the portals of Gothic churches [*375, 377, 392, 687*] or Gothic picture frames [*437*]. When relatively small, such ornaments are often called "gablets" (gay′blets).

GENRE (zhahn-ruh; F. fr. L. *genus*, kind, class). Representations of everyday life, usually restricted to those made for their own sake rather than for some religious, moral, or symbolic purpose. Genre scenes and figures are common in Hellenistic and Roman art and in Western art since the sixteenth century [*4, 183, 244*, colorplates 48, 56, *646, 652, 707, 724, 739, 747*].

GISANT (zhee-zah [nasal]; F., recumbent figure; *pl.* gisants). A tomb effigy of the deceased as a corpse. On fourteenth- and fifteenth-century Gothic tombs, the gisant was sometimes shown in a hideous state of decomposition, as a "memento mori" (reminder of death) for the living. Germain Pilon's Renaissance gisants of Catherine de' Medici and Henry II at St. Denis [*601, 602*], however, have been given an ideal beauty that evokes pathos only when we remind ourselves that such apparently noble people are now dead.

GLAZE (fr. Middle English *glasen*, fr. *glas*, glass). **1.** A glassy coat applied to pottery to seal and color it [*508*]. **2.** A thin, transparent or semi-transparent film of *oil paint* brushed over another layer of paint, allowing it to show through and usually altering its color. Thus glazes of red and flesh color laid over glazes of blue which, in turn, may be laid over a brown *underpainting* will approximate the healthy glow of living flesh, as in the paintings of Velasquez and Fragonard [colorplates 54, 57]. Opaque *impastos* and "scumbles" may be added over transparent glazes to provide *highlights* and additional shadows. Both glazing and scumbling allow lower layers of paint to show through, but in glazing, the lower layer is seen because the glaze is transparent and in scumbling, it is seen because there are breaks in the rough, opaque paint as it is dragged across the canvas [colorplates 54, 63].

GOLD GROUND. The spatially neutral background of gold leaf against which figures were placed in medieval *mosaics*, panel paintings, and *miniatures* [colorplates 13–15, 19, 20, 23]. In mosaic decoration, the gold leaf was usually applied to the back of each transparent glass *tessera*; the light is refracted as it passes into the glass, then reflected by the gold leaf, and refracted again as it passes back out through the glass. The individual reflection and refraction of light within each of the hundreds of tesserae, each set at a slightly different angle than the rest, creates a golden radiance which appears to emanate from within the wall itself and shimmers with the slightest movement of the viewer. In painting, gold leaf is attached with a pigment called "bole," usually a dull red which actually adds to the richness of the ground when the thin leaf begins to flake [colorplate 24]. In panel painting, the gold ground is frequently tooled and built up ornamentally with plaster.

GOSPEL BOOK. A book containing the four Gospels of the New Testament which tell of the life and death of Christ and are ascribed to the Evangelists Matthew, Mark, Luke, and John, respectively. In medieval Gospel books, the symbol or "portrait" of each Evangelist often appears as a frontispiece to his Gospel [*324, 326,* colorplates 17–20, *361*].

GREEK AND ROMAN TEMPLE ARCHITECTURE. *See* CELLA, MOLDING, NAOS, ORDERS, PEDIMENT, PERIPTERAL, PERISTYLE, PODIUM, PORTICO, PRONAOS, STEREOBATE, STYLOBATE, THOLOS.

GREEK VASES. *See* AMPHORA, BLACK-FIGURED, KYLIX, LEKYTHOS, RED-FIGURED.

GROUND-LINE. The single line or edge used to indicate the level of the ground in the drawings of children and in the paintings and reliefs of the Egyptians, Sumerians, Assyrians, early Greeks, etc. [*41–43, 74, 84, 92, 116, 119,* colorplate 8]. Since all figures and objects are oriented in relation to the ground-line, it is a simple but effective means of organizing a composition. Compositions with ground-lines present a marked contrast to the less precisely oriented clusters of figures in the art of younger children and prehistoric man [*12, 15, 40*]. In more advanced stages of compositional organization, more than one ground-line may be introduced for figures intended to be further back; thus there is the suggestion of a *picture space.* The ground-lines may be further elaborated by making them ripple to suggest the contours of the topography [*66, 76*] or by placing some of them obliquely to connect with other ground-lines [83].

GROUND PLANE. In a picture or relief, the surface, apparently receding into the *picture space,* upon which people and objects seem to stand [fig. 36, *478, 520*].

GUTTAE (gut′ee; *sing.* gutta; L., drops). In an *entablature* of the Doric *order,* peg-like projections beneath the *regulae* and *mutules,* possibly derived from the pegs used in wooden structures [fig. 29, *138, 139*].

HALLENKIRCHE (hahl′en-keersh′eh). The German word for "hall church," a church with *nave* and *side aisles* of equal height [*384*].

HAND. The unique *style* of a painter, sculptor, draftsman, etc, by which his work is recognized, especially in so far as it is recognizable by his *handling* of a *medium.* An artist may remain anonymous, like the "Foundry Painter" [*121*] or the "Master of the Hausbuch" [*468*], yet still have a clearly recognizable "artistic personality." The "hand" of such an artist is quickly discerned in his works. Sometimes, different hands may be distinguished within a single work, especially a *workshop* production. Much of the work of the *connoisseur* is devoted to distinguishing such hands and assigning an "oeuvre" (erv′r; F.), or body of work, to a given "master."

HANDLING. The particular way in which an artist works with his *medium.* Since the brushstrokes of a painter, the chisel strokes of a sculptor, or the pen strokes of a draughtsman may be even more personal than his handwriting, they are usually a principal means of identifying his individual *style.*

HATCHING. A series of parallel lines used in drawing and printmaking to darken, or lower the *value,* of an area. In simple parallel hatching a single set of lines is used [fig. 23a, *517, 528*]. In "crosshatching," a network of lines of darker value is made by drawing one set of hatchings over another [fig. 23b.

Fig. 23. Types of hatching.

468, 586]. An even denser network of lines, called "double cross-hatching," may be made by superimposing still another set of parallels over simple crosshatching [fig. 23c., *640*]. The roundness or *plasticity* of an object can be emphasized by "contour hatching," a series of curving lines defining the changing surfaces of three-dimensional forms [fig. 23d, *581, 583*]. By systematically varying the intervals between the lines of contour hatchings or by setting up a *foreshortened* grid of contour cross-hatchings [fig. 23e, *527*], striking effects of spatial recession can be created.

HIGHLIGHTS. Those parts of an illuminated object which reflect the most light. In all kinds of *relief sculpture* much of the illusion of space and *plasticity* results from careful control of those edges and internal surfaces which catch the light, but this is especially true of sculpture in low relief [*62, 66, 85, 229, 475*]. When *modeling* an object in a painting, the artist usually determines the location of the highlights, middle lights, and darks in reference to a point source of illumination or, in considering his composition as a whole, according to those parts he wishes to emphasize for expressive reasons. In sixteenth-century Venetian painting and in many Baroque paintings, sudden and dramatic highlights are common. Often, in these paintings, there is not only a sudden change in *value* but in the texture of the paint as well, a thick *impasto* being employed to snap the area forward [colorplates 40, 51, 54, *555, 632*]. Highlights in drawing, printmaking, and watercolor painting, however, are usually formed by leaving the white of the paper uncovered rather than by adding a light pigment [*467, 517, 527, 528, 580, 581, 584, 586, 640, 716*].

HÔTEL (oh-tel). A large French town house [*378, 670*].

HUE. That property of a color which gives it its name—red, green, violet, etc. The continuous band of the visible spectrum is usually divided into six basic hues—red, orange, yellow, green, blue, and violet—ranging from the *warm colors* to the *cool colors*. Intermediate hues can easily be described by reference to the neighboring hues, e.g. "orange-yellow," "blue-green," etc. White and black and the grays resulting from their mixture are "achromatic" colors; they are distinguished only by *value*, not by hue.

ICON (ai-kon; fr. Gk. *eikon*, image). One of the panel paintings of Christ, the Virgin, or the saints which are venerated by Orthodox Christians [*287–289*].

ILLUMINATED MANUSCRIPT. A manuscript decorated or illustrated with paintings and drawings, especially one ornamented with gold and silver and brilliant colors [colorplates 16, 17, 19, 20, 25]. *See* BOOK OF HOURS,

CALLIGRAPHY, CODEX, DRÔLERIES, GOSPEL BOOK, MINIATURE, PAPYRUS, PARCH-
MENT, PSALTER, VELLUM.

ILLUSIONISM (fr. L. *illudere*, to mock). The endeavor of artists to represent
visual phenomena as completely as possible within the limitations of their
particular *medium* and the conventions of the time. The degree of illusionism
achieved in any work cannot be measured absolutely, but only in relation to
the methods of representation already established. When the Madonnas of
Cimabue [*426*], Giotto [*431*], and Masaccio [*495*] are compared, it is
apparent that each marks a different stage of technical progress in the
recording of visual phenomena, but, in all probability, each painting
appeared strikingly lifelike at the time it was painted. (Whether or not one
is superior to another in artistic quality is another matter altogether.) When
one of the primary aims of an artist is to astonish the viewer with the apparent reality of an illusion, the French term "trompe l'oeil" (trohmp lur;
"deceive the eye") is often used to describe both the object and the act of
deception.

IMPASTO (im-pa'sto; It. *im*, in, + *pasta*, paste). Paint applied with the
consistency of a thick paste, often used by Venetian and Baroque masters in
sudden patches (impastos) of high *value* for *highlights* [colorplates 51, 54,
555, *632*, *637*, *638*]. Among more recent masters noted for their heavy
impasto are Cézanne [colorplate 66], Van Gogh [colorplate 68, *760*],
Rouault [colorplate 71], Soutine [*772*], Nolde [*774*], and Kokoschka [*775*].
Cf. GLAZE.

INSULA (in'soo-la; *pl.* insulae; in'soo-lee; L., island). **1.** A block in a Roman
city. **2.** A large building or group of buildings in a Roman city, similar to a
modern apartment house with shops on the ground floor and living quarters
above [*217*].

JAMB. The side of a doorway or window frame [fig. 45]. The jambs of the
portals of Romanesque and Gothic churches are frequently "splayed"
(beveled or spread outward) and decorated with figure sculpture [*356*,
396]. The part of the jamb from the window or door to the surface of the
wall is called the "reveal" or, if it is splayed, the "splay." Much of the effect
of mass in Romanesque architecture is due to the splays of windows and
doorways which make walls seem even thicker than they actually are [*329*,
337].

KEEP. The massive central tower of a castle, used as a dwelling place by the
lord of the castle and, in case of attack, as a final point of defense [colorplate
25]. Also called *donjon*.

KINETIC SCULPTURE. Sculpture which is made to be seen while all or part
of it is set in motion by mechanical or natural means. Many pieces of static
sculpture, however, are intended to be set into apparent motion through
the effect of parallax (apparent change in the position of objects—or parts of
objects—relative to each other when seen from different *viewpoints*) and
apparent changes in the shapes of solid and hollow *volumes* as the observer
walks around them [*181*, *183*, *514*, *569*, *570*, *671*, *800–807*]. Early forms of
kinetic sculpture (although they were not called that at the time) are

fountains, fireworks, stage machines, and automata, all of which were highly developed during the seventeenth and eighteenth centuries. Abstract sculpture made with moving metal parts became popular in the mid-twentieth century due, in large measure, to the pioneering work of Alexander Calder [*808*]. *See* MOBILE.

KOUROS (koo′ross; *pl.* kouroi; Gk., a youth). An Archaic Greek statue of a standing nude youth [*124, 125*]. The Archaic Greek statues of clothed maidens [*129*, colorplate 6] are known as "korai" (*sing.* kore; kor′ay).

KYLIX (kai′lix; *pl.* kylikes; kai′lih-keez). An ancient Greek drinking cup with two horizontal handles near the rim of a broad, shallow bowl standing on a slender stem with a relatively small foot [fig. 24, *120–122*].

LANTERN. 1. A turret crowning a dome, roof, or tower, usually pierced with windows for light or louvres for ventilation [fig. 18, *280, 343, 546, 663, 675, 682*]. **2.** A tower above the *crossing* of a church [*334, 379*].

Fig. 24. (Sixth century B.C.).

LAPIS LAZULI (lap′is laz′yoolee). A semiprecious blue stone found in the Near East, used for carving and pulverized to make true ultramarine blue, a very intense and expensive pigment used by medieval and Renaissance artists, especially for painting the robe of the Virgin [colorplates 26, 29].

LEKYTHOS (lek′ih-thos; *pl.* lekythoi). A nearly cylindrical ancient Greek oil flask, tapered at the bottom, with a slender vertical handle springing from a rather flat shoulder and attached to a long narrow neck with a small mouth for pouring (fig. 25). "White-ground" lekythoi, covered with a yellowish-white slip and often decorated with delicate brush drawings of domestic scenes and scenes of farewell, were used as funerary offerings [*166*].

LINE. In drawing, a mark left by a moving point. Since we are all familiar, to some degree, with the varieties of line made by different movements of

Fig. 25.

the hand, lines are often evocative of states of feeling associated with those movements. Thus, lines are frequently described as nervous, gentle, strong, angry, tense, etc. Variations in direction, thickness, and density may record the sudden movements and pressures usually required to make a jagged line or the gentle and relaxed motions required to draw a light, undulating line with any rapidity [cf. *166, 167, 326, 327, 770, 771, 832*]. The outlines, silhouettes, or edges of objects are also often called "lines." Although such "lines" may not actually have been made by a moving point they often have much of the same character. Sometimes, a painting—and even a sculpture or a building—with few or no lines drawn on its surface, is described as "linear," if its edges are sharply defined [*351, 451, 501*]. In any work, linear or not, lines may be implied by separate edges or points brought into alignment with each other [fig. 43]. The eye quickly relates these separate elements; children, for example, in connecting the numbered points in a follow-the-dots picture, often lose interest and put down their pencils once the direction of the "line" established by the dots becomes clear.

LINTEL (lin′tul). A horizontal beam, of any material, spanning an opening, as over a window or doorway, or between two pillars [fig. 37, *23, 60, 111*]. The lintels of the portals of Romanesque and Gothic churches are often highly ornamented [fig. 45, *351, 354, 396*]. *See* POST-AND-LINTEL CONSTRUCTION.

LITHOGRAPH (fr. Gk. *lithos*, stone, + *graphein*, to write). A print made from a design drawn on a slab of fine-grained limestone. The lithographic process is based on the principle that water and grease will not mix. The design is drawn on the flat surface of the stone with greasy lithographic crayons or pencils, or with a pen or brush dipped in lithographic ink (tusche). Sometimes, a plate of zinc or some other metal, which has been given a granulated surface that will hold both grease and water, is used instead. Once the surface is moistened with water, the greasy printing ink, which is rolled over it, will only adhere to the greasy lines of the drawing. Prints are made by placing a dampened sheet of paper on top of the stone or plate, and passing them, on a traveling bed, through a special press which rubs the back of the paper. Any of the common drawing techniques can be used in making a lithograph; no special style or technical skill is required of the artist as in the preparation of a *woodcut, engraving,* or *etching.* If the artist does not choose to be burdened with a plate or heavy stone, all he needs is a piece of paper and a lithographic crayon; later, his drawing can be directly transferred to the stone and it will not even be reversed in printing as in the other graphic processes. Unless such special effects as scratching are used, a lithograph is easily mistaken for an original drawing; only the flat and even character of the ink betray it as a print. Lithography was invented at the end of the eighteenth century and was widely used during the nineteenth century for magazine and book illustration [*723*]; it remains, in one form or another, an important means of commercial book production, since thousands of impressions can be made from a single plate.

LOGGIA (lo′ja *or* lah′ja). A covered passage or gallery with an open arcade or colonnade on one or more sides. It may be an integral part of a building, connect two separate buildings, or stand alone [*199, 544, 565, 571, 623, 675*].

LUNETTE (loo-net′; F., little moon). Any semicircular opening or surface, as on the wall of a vaulted room, over a doorway, window, etc. [*487, 508, 509, 606, 681, 684*]. A lunette over the portal to a medieval church is called a *tympanum.*

MADRASAH (ma-dras′a; Arabic, place of study). A collegiate mosque, or theological school, usually built with a vaulted hall opening onto each side of a square court with a fountain in the center [*301*].

MASTABA (mas′ta-ba; Arabic, a stone bench). A rectangular Egyptian tomb with a flat roof and "battered" (sloping) walls, covering a subterranean burial chamber and containing a chapel for offerings and a compartment, called the "serdab," with a statue of the deceased [*44*].

MEDIUM (*pl.* mediums *or* media). **1.** The physical material with which an artist works (marble, clay, ink, oil paint, steel, concrete, etc.). In creating a work of art, an artist usually "thinks in terms of his medium," attempting only what can be conveniently achieved within its physical limitations. Sometimes, however, he may display his skill in a technical "tour de force," which defies the intrinsic nature of his medium and wins applause for its sheer difficulty, quite apart from any expressive power the work may have [*243, 383, 445, 463, 581, 610, 621, 735*]. Beginning in the nineteenth century and continuing far into the twentieth century, a purist aesthetic based on "truth to material" and the "expression of structure" spread with moral fervor from architectural criticism to the criticism of the other arts; only certain forms were thought proper to a given medium: massive, chunky forms in stone sculpture, for example, or a neutral grid pattern "expressing" the steel skeleton in skyscraper design. Such limitations can be a spur to creation, as in the work of Mondrian [colorplate 76], Brancusi [*799*], Henry Moore [*800, 801*], or Mies van der Rohe [*824*], but, as Henry Moore himself has pointed out, if "truth to material" were the sole criterion of excellence, "a snowman made by a child would have to be praised at the expense of a Rodin or a Bernini." **2.** The fluid, or "vehicle," in which *pigment* is suspended to make paint, allowing it to spread easily and adhere to a surface. The medium of *oil paint* may be one of various drying oils; gum and water is the usual medium of *watercolors;* egg yolk and water is the medium for egg *tempera*, etc. The same pigments may usually be mixed with many different mediums.

MEGALITHIC (fr. Gk. *megas*, large, + *lithos*, stone). Made of great stones, as prehistoric *cromlechs* and *dolmens* [*21, 22, 23*]. Each huge stone in such a structure can be called a "megalith."

MEGARON (meg′a-ron; *pl.* megarons *or* megara; fr. *megas*, large). A large oblong hall in a Minoan or Mycenaean palace, having a hearth at the center and four columns supporting the roof. Entry to the hall was gained by first passing through a porch with two columns and then a *vestibule* [*100, 112*]. The megaron is thought to be the antecedent of the *naos* and *pronaos* of the Greek temple.

METOPE (met′oh-pee; Gk., fr. *meta*, between, + *ope*, opening). In the *frieze* of an *entablature* of the Doric *order*, one of the panels between the *triglyphs*, sometimes ornamented [*131, 138, 143, 146, 529, 684, 685*]. Originally, in wooden temples, the metopes may have been openings between the ceiling beams.

MEZZANINE (meh′za-neen; F., fr. It. *mezzanino*, fr. *mezzano*, middle). A low story between two higher ones, especially one just above the ground floor [*810, 811*].

MIHRAB (mee′rahb; Arabic). A niche on the wall of a mosque, indicating the *qibla* or direction of Mecca [*295, 296*].

MINARET (min-a-ret′). One of the towers of a mosque, tall and slender in its developed form and ringed with one or more balconies from which the muezzin (moo-ez′in) calls the faithful to prayer [*274, 294, 302–304*].

MINIATURE (fr. Medieval L. *miniatura*, fr. *miniare*, to color with minium, a red pigment used for illuminating manuscripts). **1.** Any painting or drawing in an *illuminated manuscript* [*261, 438*, colorplates 17, 19, 20, 25]. **2.** A very small portrait intended as a keepsake [*251, 459, 591*].

MOBILE (moh′beel). A delicately balanced construction of movable parts made to be suspended in such a way that the parts will be set in motion by movements of the air. Alexander Calder was the first to make this form of *kinetic sculpture* [*808*].

MODELING. **1.** The creation of three-dimensional forms by working some soft material such as clay. Modeling is often an additive process; it differs from the entirely subtractive process of carving in that material may be added as well as taken away. **2.** By analogy, in painting and drawing, the suggestion of the three-dimensional character of a body by altering the *value* of colors along its surface, as though light were falling with greater intensity on some parts than on others. In painting, this may be accomplished by applying *shades* and *tints* of the basic *hue*. Sometimes, however, the basic hue is used at its highest *saturation* for the lowest dark, while tints of the same hue are used for the rest of the area being modeled. In this case, the colors are more luminous since none of them are deadened by mixture with black, but the darks, because of their higher saturation, may be more insistent than the lights. The darks, then, will tend to project and may counteract, to a degree, the effect of *plasticity* which is usually the purpose of modeling in the first place [colorplate 23, 24, 31]. In "color modeling," used extensively by Cézanne [colorplate 66], the tendency of *cool colors* to recede and *warm colors* to project, is exploited; reds, oranges, and yellows are used to bring *planes* forward and blues to keep them back in the *picture space*. Color modeling is usually used as a supplement to traditional modeling rather than as a total replacement for it. *See* SHADING.

MODULE (mod′yool). The basic unit of measure determining the major divisions and *proportions* of an object, figure, building, or site.

MOLDING. An ornamental band of grooves or projections which lend intricacy to the surfaces of buildings by catching and modulating the light and casting shadows. Complex moldings are usually compounded of a few basic and familiar forms [figs. 26, 27]. Moldings, whether used singly or as members of a compound molding, may be smooth and continuous or have their surfaces "enriched" with carving. In classical architecture, only certain types of ornament are customarily applied to certain types of molding, because of the particular affinities of form between the ornaments and the *profiles* of the moldings. The "egg-and-dart" *motif*, for example, is usually

Fig. 26. Corinthian capital and entablature after Palladio.

(a) Cyma recta molding with interlaced dolphins, forming the "cymatium," or top member of the cornice.

(b) Cyma reversa molding with leaf-and-dart motif.

(c) Fascia enriched with fluting.

(d) Cyma reversa molding with leaf ornament.

(e) Modillions with acanthus leaf ornament.

(f) Ovolo molding with egg-and-dart motif.

(g) Dentils.

(h) Cyma reversa molding with leaf ornament.

(i) Frieze with rinceau of acanthus leaves.

(j) Fillet molding.

(k) Cyma reversa molding with acanthus ornament.

(l) Astragal molding with bead-and-reel motif.

(m) Fascia.

(n) Cyma reversa molding with leaf ornament.

(o) Fascia.

(p) Astragal molding with bead-and-reel motif.

(q) Fascia.

(r) Ovolo molding, which, together with (s), forms the abacus of the capital.

(s) Cavetto molding with acanthus flower.

(t) Volute.

(u) Acanthus leaves on the bell of the capital.

(v) Astragal molding.

applied to the ovolo molding, the "leaf-and-dart" to the cyma reversa, and the "bead-and-reel" to the astragal, etc. [fig. 26, *133, 229, 508, 509, 516*].

MONASTERY (fr. Gk. *monasterion,* a place for living alone). The dwelling place of a community of monks. The many parts of a large monastery are indicated in fig. 28, based on a ninth-century plan preserved in the library of the monastery of St. Gall, Switzerland [*cf. 323*]. The monks slept in the "dormitory," ate in the "refectory," copied manuscripts in the "scriptorium," lodged guests in the "hostelry," distributed alms in the "almonry," nursed the sick in the "infirmary," and in the

Fig. 27. Column base after Serlio: (a) torus molding with guilloche ornament, (b) scotia molding, (c) torus molding with leaf garland, (d) plinth with Vitruvian scroll.

"novitiate"—itself a monastery in miniature—instructed the novices in the monastic life.

MONUMENTAL. An adjective frequently used in art criticism to describe any structure, painting, figure, etc., which is grand, massive and apparently permanent like a monument, regardless of its actual size. The term is also used to describe any work that is merely large, even though it may be small in intrinsic *scale*.

MOSAIC. A method of decorating walls, pavements, and vaults with patterns or pictures composed of small pieces of colored stone or glass (*tesserae*) set in a wet cement which, upon hardening, holds them in place. Mosaics were widely used in ancient Roman houses and Early Christian and Byzantine churches [*243, 256, 259, 260, 270, 271, 279, 281, 284, 285, 292,* colorplates 13–15]. *See* GOLD GROUND.

MOSQUE ARCHITECTURE. *See* MADRASAH, MIHRAB, MINARET, QIBLA, STALACTITE.

MOTIF (moh-teef'). **1.** Any prominent feature of the *subject* or form of a work of art. **2.** The natural landscape serving as the subject of a landscape painting. The Impressionists made a point of painting "en plein air" (in the open air), directly from the motif, rather than in the studio from sketches [colorplate 65, *744*].

MURAL (fr. L. *murus,* wall). A large painting, in any *medium,* made for a particular wall, whether painted directly on its surface or painted on a canvas or panel affixed to it. *Cf.* FRESCO.

MUTULE (myoo'chool). One of a series of flat blocks with *guttae* under the projecting *cornice* of an *entablature* of the Doric *order* [*131, 138, 143, 144*].

NAOS (nay'os). The Greek word for the *cella,* or main body, of a temple [*137*].

NARTHEX. The entrance hall or porch preceding the *nave* of a church. In churches with an *atrium,* the narthex is often simply one side of the open

Fig. 28. (Porter).

35

ambulatory [*254, 343*]. At Hagia Sophia there is an outer narthex (exonarthex) in addition to the main narthex [*273*].

NAVE (nayv, fr. L. *navis*, a ship). The great central space in a church. In longitudinal churches, it extends from the entrance to the *apse* (or only to the *crossing* or *choir*, when these exist) and is usually flanked by *side aisles* [fig. 10, *254*].

ODALISQUE (oh'da-lisk; F., ohda-leesk'). A female harem slave. The reclining odalisque was as popular a *subject* for nineteenth-century French painters as the reclining Venus for Renaissance and Baroque masters [*721*, colorplate 60].

OIL PAINTING. Although Jan van Eyck is traditionally credited with the invention of oil painting, *pigments* mixed with drying oils (linseed, walnut, poppyseed, etc.) were used long before the fifteenth century for special purposes such as painting on stone or metal. Van Eyck and the Master of Flémalle, however, were among the first to use the medium for ordinary panel painting. With oils, which were far more flexible than the traditional *tempera*, they could create *illusionistic* effects of extraordinary subtlety, richness, and luminosity [colorplates 27, 28]. Oils permitted the smooth blending of colors, high *saturation* even at low *values*, the use of transparent *glazes*, almost infinite detail, and the possibility of reworking the same area over and over again. Other capabilities of oil paint were realized in the sixteenth and seventeenth centuries, when it was sometimes roughly applied to coarse canvas in opaque "scumbles" and thick *impastos*, or mixed on the canvas with wet paint of another *hue* to create "shot colors" [colorplate 54]. Oils are usually applied either to a panel covered with layers of smooth "gesso" (plaster of Paris), as in tempera painting, or to stretched canvas primed with a mixture of glue and white pigment. When the paint is dry, a coat of varnish may be applied to protect the surface and to brighten and blend the colors. Since varnish will yellow in time, it must be periodically dissolved and renewed if the colors are to retain a semblance of their original appearance.

ORDERS. An architectural "order" is one of the classical systems of carefully proportioned and interdependent parts which include a *column* (comprised of base, shaft, and *capital*) and its *entablature* (comprised of *architrave, frieze,* and *cornice*). Although the capital of each of the five generally recognized orders is its most distinctive feature, each order also has its own characteristic system of *proportion*, so that any alteration in the size of one part necessitates a change in the size of all the other parts [fig. 29]. The oldest, sturdiest, and most severe of the orders are the Greek Doric [*131, 138–146*], which is the only order without a base, and the Tuscan, which is supposedly derived from ancient Etruscan temples [*194*]. The Roman Doric, while it has a frieze composed of *triglyphs* and *metopes* like the Greek Doric, differs from it in having a base [*529, 684*]. The Ionic order is more slender than the Tuscan or Doric and is quickly distinguished by the *volutes* of its capital; like the Corinthian and Composite orders, it has a three-part architrave [*138, 150, 178, 200, 573*]. The Corinthian [fig. 26, *149, 151, 201, 219, 617, 618*] and

Fig. 29. The Tuscan, Roman Doric, Ionic, Corinthian, and Composite orders after Scamozzi: (A) cornice, (B) frieze, (C) architrave, (D) capital, (E) shaft, (F) base, (G) cap, (H) die, (I) plinth; (A), (B), (C) comprise the entablature; (D), (E), (F) the column; (G), (H), (I) the pedestal.

37

Composite [*218*, bottom; *256, 574*] orders are the most sumptuously ornamented and the most slender; both have capitals decorated with *acanthus*
leaves, but in the capital of the Composite order the leaves are combined with
the large volutes of the Ionic order. The pedestals, which are sometimes used
to support the columns of an order, are not considered part of the order
itself, but architectural theorists since the Renaissance have provided
appropriate proportions and *moldings* for pedestals for each of the orders
[fig. 29]. Pedestals are useful devices for raising an order above a *balustrade*
[*208, 675, 693*] or for raising the entablature above a row of windows [*545*]
or above the crowns of the arches of an "arch order" (an order applied to
an *arch* or arcade) [*241, 503, 598, 660*] without altering the width of the
columns. If, in these cases, the columns were placed lower down, but allowed
to rise to the same height, they would have to be thicker, because the proportion of each column is predetermined. In some cases, one of the more
slender orders might be used to reach the same height without a corresponding increase in width, but the choice of another order would change the
character of the building. The ornate Composite order, for example, would
hardly be an appropriate substitute for the Tuscan if the architect had already fixed on just this order as the means of conveying an impression of a
stern, martial character. Once a particular order has been selected, the
classical or classicizing architect must abide by its traditionally accepted set
of proportions. He cannot simply stretch or compress the shafts of his columns
at will as Romanesque and Gothic architects chose to do [*335, 341, 351,
367, 369*]. *Also see* ABACUS, ATTIC, CARYATID, COLOSSAL ORDER, ECHINUS,
ENTASIS, FLUTING, GUTTAE, MODULE, MUTULE, PILASTER, REGULA, RESPOND,
SUPERIMPOSED ORDERS, TAENIA.

PAINTING MEDIA AND TECHNIQUES. *See* CARTOON, ENCAUSTIC, FRESCO,
GLAZE, GOLD GROUND, IMPASTO, MEDIUM, OIL PAINTING, PIGMENT, SINOPIA,
TEMPERA, UNDERPAINTING, WASH, WATERCOLOR.

PALAZZO (pa-lot'so; *pl.* palazzi; pa-lot'see). A large Italian town house
[*491, 501, 620*].

PAPYRUS (pap-ire'-us; L. root of "paper"). A writing material of thin
sheets made by slicing and pressing the pith of the papyrus plant of the Nile
Valley, used in scroll form by the ancient Egyptians, Greeks, and Romans.
Schematized versions of the papyrus plant, its bud, and its flower [*55*] were
used as models for many Egyptian *columns* and *capitals* [*47*].

PARCHMENT (fr. Gk. Pergamum, the name of a city in Asia Minor). Any
animal skin (sheep, goat, calf, etc.) prepared for writing or painting upon,
including *vellum* [colorplates 17, 19, 20].

PASTEL. Powdered pigments mixed with gum and formed into sticks for
drawing. Pastels are usually so broadly applied over the entire surface of
the paper that the effect resembles oil painting, although the colors are
generally rather pale and have a dusty look. The medium was popular with
eighteenth- and nineteenth-century artists, especially in France. Degas was
able to achieve unusually rich effects by roughly *hatching* one layer of intense
color over another [*742, 743*]. **2.** An adjective used to describe colors, in any
medium, that are pale like pastels [colorplate 58].

PAVILION (fr. F. *pavillion*, a tent). **1.** Any light, ornamental building [*688*]. **2.** Any large-scale block or wing of a building projecting from the main body [*598, 622, 659, 693*].

PEDIMENT (ped'iment). **1.** In classical architecture, the low-pitched *gable*, or triangular area, formed by the two slopes of the low-pitched roof of a temple, framed by the horizontal and raking *cornices* and sometimes filled with sculpture [*130, 131, 133, 134, 200, 210, 503, 573, 663, 675, 677, 682, 684, 685*]. **2.** Any architectural member of similar shape, as over a door, niche, window, etc. [*505, 574, 681*]; sometimes, the upper cornice takes the curve of a segment of a circle, in which case it is called a "segmental pediment" [*541, 542, 598, 622, 674, 693*]. "Broken pediments," having parts of their cornices omitted or brought forward in advance of other sections, were sometimes used in later Roman and Baroque architecture [*218, 545, 572, 577, 611*].

PENDENTIVE (pen-den'tiv; fr. L. *pendere*, to hang). One of the curving triangular segments of *vaulting* which spring from the corners of a square plan to support a circular *dome* or *drum* [fig. 18, *281, 506, 676*], first used on a large scale at Hagia Sophia [*272, 273, 276*].

PERIPTERAL (peh-rip'teral). An adjective describing a building with a colonnade around its entire perimeter [*137–145, 178, 179, 529, 530*]. The "Maison Carrée" at Nîmes and the "Temple of Fortuna Virilis" at Rome [*200*] are "pseudo-peripteral" in that the columns around the *cella* are engaged (set in the wall) and not free-standing.

PERISTYLE (perry'-style; fr. Gk. *peri*, around, + *stylos*, a column). **1.** The colonnade around a *peripteral* building [*137*] or around a court [*530*]. **2.** An open garden court in a Roman house, surrounded by a colonnade [fig. 19].

PERSPECTIVE. The representation, on a two-dimensional surface, of three-dimensional objects in space. The term is sometimes restricted to the particular method of spatial representation developed during the fifteenth century, in which all parallel lines and edges of surfaces receding at the same angle are drawn, on the *picture plane*, in such a way that they converge toward a single *vanishing point* [figs. 30a, 30b, 47, *477, 478, 492, 493, 495, 497–499, 516, 518, 520, 524, 550, 559, 578, 586, 611, 617, 625, 678, 709*]. This method of suggesting a single unified space is often called "linear perspective" to distinguish it from the many other methods of spatial representation which were developed long before the Renaissance. It is a highly artificial system presupposing a one-eyed observer standing stock still and staring dead ahead, but it has important advantages: a high degree of artistic focus and unity can be achieved because all receding surfaces are usually related to only one or two vanishing points; when only one vanishing point is used, it may be located within the principal figure or at some other significant *focal point* within the composition; a single *viewpoint* can be precisely established so that the *picture space* appears to be a continuation of the actual space in which the viewer stands; and, if the rate of diminution in the size of objects and the intervals between them is kept absolutely regular as they recede toward the background, the size of all similar objects can be precisely determined once the size of only one of them is known. In practice, however,

Fig. 30a. Perspective diagram of Masaccio's "Trinity" fresco in S. Maria Novella, Florence.

Fig. 30b. Diagrams deduced from Masaccio's "Trinity" showing the ground plan of the chamber and the surface of the barrel vault (H. W. Janson).

even Renaissance artists seldom used the new invention with complete consistency; it took a great deal of time to apply the system with mathematical exactitude and strict adherence to it might even conflict with more important artistic concerns. At any rate, a very convincing illusion of space could be achieved if the older means of spatial representation were included within only a general framework constructed according to the new system. Among these older means of suggesting depth are: (1) "vertical perspective,"

in which objects farther from the observer are shown higher on the picture plane than those which are closer [fig. 31, *66, 67, 76, 262, 311,* colorplates 13, 77, *831*]; (2) "diagonal perspective," in which farther objects are not only higher on the picture plane than nearer objects but are also aligned along an oblique *axis,* thereby suggesting continuous recession [fig. 32, *83, 233, 288, 289, 327, 363, 439, 829, 834*]; (3) overlapping [fig. 33, *55, 56, 58, 62, 65, 84, 105, 119, 266, 271, 362,* colorplates 4, 20]; (4) diminution in the size of objects and diminution of the interval between them according to

Fig. 31. Figures arranged in "vertical perspective."

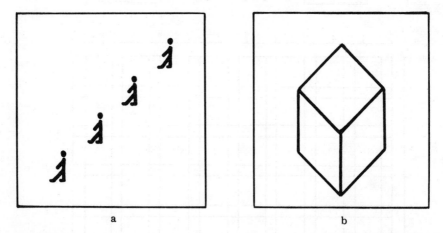

a
                                b

Fig. 32. (a) Figures arranged in "diagonal perspective." (b) Cube represented in "diagonal perspective."

their distance from the viewer [figs. 23e, 34, colorplates 9, 25, *261, 433, 434*]; (5) *foreshortening* [fig. 22, *121, 185, 198, 244*]; (6) *modeling* [*249, 250, 251, 287,* colorplate 11, *324–326, 425*]; (7) cast *shadows* [fig. 41, *243, 245, 247,* colorplates 12, 25, 28, *443, 447*]; (8) *atmospheric perspective* [*246, 248,* colorplates 9, 27]. Each one of these "distal cues," or signs of spatial recession, may be used alone or in various combinations. All of them are either

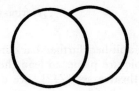

Fig. 33. Recession by overlapping.

Fig. 34. Recession by diminution of size and interval.

already included and refined within the system of linear perspective or can be combined with it to enhance the illusion of depth. They can also be combined with those earlier systems in which the parallel lines of receding surfaces converge in several unrelated vanishing points [*246, 427–429, 441*], along a "vanishing axis" [fig. 35, color-plate 24, *426*], or in a "vanishing area" [*431, 432,* colorplate 28, *449*].

PIAZZA (pee-at′-sa). Italian word for a public square [*393, 394, 607, 619*], called a "place" (plahss) in France, a "Platz" (plahtz) in Germany and Austria, and a "plaza" (plah′tha) in Spain.

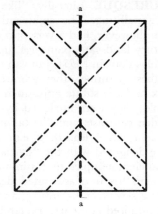

Fig. 35. Orthogonals converging along a "vanishing axis" (a).

PICTURE PLANE. The surface upon which a picture is painted [fig. 36, *586*].

PICTURE SPACE. The space that appears to extend back beyond a *picture plane*, although it is only an illusion created by such pictorial devices as *foreshortening*, linear *perspective*, and *atmospheric perspective* [fig. 36, *586*]. For ease in describing the location of objects on the *ground plane*, the picture space is usually divided into "foreground," "middle ground," and "background." Any object or figure in the extreme foreground which is used to lead the eye into the picture and to "push back" other objects, making them appear farther back in the picture space than they otherwise would, is called a "repoussoir" (ruh-poo-swahr; F. fr. *repousser*, to push back) [*428, 430, 559,*

Fig. 36. Transparent cube showing picture plane (a), picture space (b), ground plane (c), orthogonals (O), and transversals (T).

635, 640, 739, 740, 762]. Planes which are established further back in the picture space and are placed parallel to the picture plane, to lead the eye back like the stage flats on either side of a theater set [*742*], are called "coulisses" (koo-leess), the French word for such side-scenes or "wings" [colorplates 9, 36, 37, *727, 758*].

PICTURESQUE. Literally, "like a picture" or providing a suitable subject for a painting. The eighteenth-century British gentlemen who used the term, however, had a very particular kind of painting in mind: seventeenth-century landscape paintings such as those by Claude Lorraine [*656, 657*], Nicolas Poussin [*655*], Jan van Goyen [*641*], and Jacob van Ruisdael [*642*]. In these paintings, they admired the broad handling of areas of light and dark and the subtle adjustment, or "keeping," of values in relation to the whole; they were intrigued by the "intricacy" of outline and texture, the sudden contrasts and "irritations" of the eye, the irregular "grouping" of elements which lead the eye gradually back into hazy "distances;" and they were delighted with the "partial concealment" of Gothic ruins, old castles, or ancient temples that stimulated curiosity and roused the imagination through "trains of associated ideas." These effects, which the British admired in the seventeenth-century landscape paintings which they collected, they also admired in the natural landscape around them. They saw the landscape of England, Scotland, and Wales with eyes accustomed to the effects of Baroque painting and, not content simply to travel in search of the Picturesque and to describe it, as the Rev. William Gilpin did in his "Picturesque Tours," or to write poems about it as John Dyer and James Thompson did, they "improved" their country estates to bring them into harmony with the effects of the landscape painting which they admired. In the process, they created the "English garden," or "landscape garden," and provided an alternative to the formal gardens of the school of Le Nôtre [*661*].

Architecture, too, was viewed with the painter's eye and analogies were drawn with landscape painting. James Adam, brother of Robert Adam [*683*], noted: "What is so material an excellence in landscape is not less requisite for composition in architecture, namely the variety of contour, a rise and fall of the different parts and likewise those great projections and recesses which produce a broad light and shade." These qualities were considered essential to the creation of "movement." Movement in architecture, like movement in landscape, involves, as Robert Adam put it, "an agreeable and diversified contour, that groups and contrasts like a picture." Any building, then, which displays such movement is Picturesque, i.e. it has qualities similar to those of a Baroque landscape painting. Toward the end of the eighteenth century, admirers of the Picturesque went so far as to model their buildings on the *asymmetrical* villas and castles depicted in the landscapes of Claude and Poussin, so that they too would blend into their surroundings and create a variety of interesting angle views. Not surprisingly, Sir John Vanbrugh, the first Englishman to design intentionally irregular buildings and one of the first to conceive the landscape garden, was also the architect who was most highly praised throughout the eighteenth century for his handling of movement [*677*]. Reynolds called him "an architect who composed like a Painter" and praised him for his skill in "affecting the imagination by means of association of ideas," a psychological factor that is almost inseparable from the Picturesque point of view, despite the high value that the enthusiasts of the Picturesque placed on the appreciation of abstract form. Reynolds explains the principle of association by offering an example which is particularly relevant to Vanbrugh's architecture:

> Thus, for instance, as we have naturally a veneration for antiquity, whatever building brings to our remembrance ancient customs and manners, such as the Castles of the Barons of ancient Chivalry, is sure to give delight. Hence it is that *towers and battlements* are so often selected by the Painter and the Poet, to make a part of the composition of their ideal Landscape; and it is from hence in a great degree, that in the buildings of Vanbrugh, who was a Poet as well as an Architect, there is a greater display of imagination, than we shall find perhaps in any other. . . For the purpose, Vanbrugh appears to have had recourse to some of the principles of the Gothick Architecture; which, though not so ancient as the Grecian, is more so to our imagination. . ." (Discourse XIII)

It is chiefly the principle of association—especially, the evocation of the ancient and the exotic [*686, 688, 692*]—for which the Picturesque is remembered today; the importance of the Picturesque point of view in the evolution of abstract art and the direct dependence of twentieth-century site planning and asymmetrical architectural design upon the Picturesque [*813–819, 826–828*] has only recently been acknowledged.

PIER (peer). Any vertical mass of masonry such as the supporting members of an arcade [figs. 1, 52].

PIGMENT. The powder which gives paint its color, obtained from any of a great variety of clays, stones, animal and vegetable matter, synthetic dyes, etc. To make paint, pigments are mixed with a "vehicle," or *medium* (glue, egg, oil, etc.), which allows the color to be easily spread and fixed to a surface.

PILASTER (pil-ass'ter). A flat, vertical member projecting slightly from a wall surface and divided, like a *column* of one of the classical *orders*, into a base, shaft, and *capital* [*199, 218, 501, 503, 505, 509, 545*]. Pilasters, although they customarily support an *entablature*, are usually introduced for decorative rather than structural reasons. The pilaster-like shafts projecting from the exterior walls of Romanesque churches, often without bases or capitals, are called "pilaster strips" to distinguish them from pilasters of the classical orders [*329, 343, 345*].

PILLAR. Any vertical support, a general term including *column, pilaster,* and *pier.*

PINNACLE (pin'a-kul; fr. L. *pinna*, a sharp point). A small ornamental turret placed, in Gothic architecture, atop *buttresses* and *piers* [fig. 52, *346, 375–377, 379, 392, 393, 432*]. Although in some cases pinnacles may load buttresses and thereby help to counteract the *thrust* of *vaults*, they are primarily decorative, contributing to the splendid confusion of the exterior, breaking horizontal lines, and, like spearheads, emphasizing the vertical sweep of Gothic design. Just as pinnacles break the silhouette of the main body of a Gothic church and point heavenward, their own surfaces may be covered with pointed gablets (little *gables*), their edges may be broken with sprouting crockets, and the whole topped with a *finial*.

PLAN (fr. L. *planum*, a flat surface). **1.** A drawing representing those parts of a building or site that would lie on a horizontal plane cutting through the building close to the floor or the ground. Doorways, windows, staircases, domes, vaults, etc., which lie above or below this plane, are usually included in the plan [*258*, cf. *256*, *257*; *273*, cf. *272*, *274*, *276*]. See ELEVATION, SECTION. **2.** The general arrangement of the parts of a building, a group of buildings, or site. Basic types of regular plans are: (1) the axial or longitudinal plan, arranged along a single *axis* [*61*, *112*, *137*] or arranged along a principal axis with parallel and transverse axes [*205*, *254*, *321*, *340*, *380*]; (2) the central plan, arranged about a single point, as in circular plans [*22*, *258*, *530*], polygonal plans [*268*, *320*, *490*], and Greek Cross plans [*505*]; (3) the grid plan, two sets of parallel axes set at right angles to each other with neither dominating [*44*]. Various combinations of these regular plans have been used [*305*, *390*, *531*, *664*] and, since the eighteenth century, intentionally irregular plans have also been cultivated [*686*, *688*, *814*, *815*, *819*,].

PLANE. A flat surface. In creating works of art and in analyzing them, it is often convenient to reduce complex three-dimensional bodies—whether a single object, figure, or an entire composition—to a few basic planes or facets. Sometimes this is done to establish the basic structure of what will be a very complicated work when it is finished, as in "blocking out" a sculpture or making a rough sketch for a painting or building [*2*, *3*, *528*, *586*; cf. *516* and *517*, cf. *713* and *714*], but often a painter or sculptor is content with a simplification of natural form [*26*, *37*, *51*, *53*, *99*, *127*, *189*]. He may even make it one of the principal aims of his art [colorplates 32, 33, 66, 67, 69, *767*, *799*]. Some architects, too, prefer smooth surfaces and simple geometrical forms [*48*, *59*, *329*, *349*, *385–391*, *505*, *815–828*].

PLASTICITY (fr. Gk. *plastos*, formed, molded). In the visual arts, the three-dimensional quality of a form, its roundness, palpability, apparent solidity, or quality of relief.

PODIUM (L., fr. Gk. *podion*, little foot). **1.** The high platform serving as a base for an Etruscan or Roman temple [*194*, *200*]. **2.** The ground floor of a building treated so that it resembles such a base [*573*, *659*, *681*].

PORTICO (por'tiko). A porch treated in the classical manner, with a colonnade supporting an *entablature* and *pediment*, usually approached by a wide flight of steps [*139*, *200*, *210*, *573*, *622*, *681*, *682*, *684*].

POST-AND-LINTEL SYSTEM. The simple and very ancient system of construction in which the basic unit consists of two or more uprights, or "posts," supporting a horizontal beam, or *lintel* [*22*, *23*]. Across two lintels, laid parallel to each other, other lintels may be laid at right angles to support a roof or ceiling; this is basically the system of the Egyptian temple [fig. 37, *59*, *60*]. When stone lintels are used, however, the supports must be close together because of the brittleness of stone, which lacks tensile strength

Fig. 37. (Chipiez).

(the ability to resist bending and stretching), although it has great strength under compression. When blocks of stone are supported throughout their length, as in a wall, they can bear a tremendous weight placed directly above them [*199*], but when a stone lintel is used to span an opening it may sag in the middle, causing the top to be squeezed shorter and the bottom to be stretched [fig. 38]. If the supports are very widely spaced, the lintel will crack and collapse of its own weight even if nothing is placed on top of it. No large hall, then, can be covered with a post-and-lintel system of stone unless the supports are placed close together, as in the many-pillared hall of an Egyptian temple, called the "hypostyle" hall (fr. Gk. *hypostylos,* resting on pillars, fr. *hypo,* under, + *stylos,* a pillar) [fig. 39, *61*]. The sanctuary, or *cella,* of a Greek temple [*137*], however, is not cluttered with columns because the roof beams were made of wood, which has much greater tensile strength than stone and therefore can be used to span much greater distances without bending and breaking. The Romans were able to cover vast, uninterrupted spaces by using an "arcuated" system, i.e. one employing the principle of the *arch,* which utilizes the high compressive strength of stone

Fig. 38. Exaggeration of stretching of the lower part of a lintel and compression of the upper part due to the pull of gravity.

without overstraining its low tensile strength. However, they retained the post-and-lintel system, or "trabeated" system (fr. L. *trabs,* beam) as it is sometimes called, for the visual *articulation* of walls [*200*] and arcades [*208*]. The post-and-lintel system is still widely used for construction in wood, steel, and *ferroconcrete* which are all high in tensile strength [*811, 824*].

PREDELLA (pray-del'la; *pl.* predellas *or* predelle; It., kneeling-stool). The base of a large *altarpiece,* frequently decorated with painted "predella panels" or sculpture expanding the theme of the major panel or panels above [colorplate 26, *443, 463*].

PRIMARY COLORS. The three basic *hues*—red, yellow, and blue—from which, theoretically, all others can be mixed. When strong color contrast is desired the primaries are often juxtaposed and used in conjunction with their *complementary colors* [colorplates 12, 16, 23, 24, 46, 60, 62–64, 69, 71, 73]. *See* SECONDARY COLORS.

PRINTMAKING. *See* WOODCUT, BLOCK BOOK, ENGRAVING, BURIN, DRYPOINT, ETCHING, LITHOGRAPH, HATCHING.

PROFILE. 1. The side view of an object. Profile and *frontal* views of objects are usually preferred in the early stages of the development of the representational arts, and frequently long after, because they reveal objects in their most characteristic aspect, without *foreshortening*. This makes them clearly recognizable and gives them an air of permanence [*17, 43, 92, 105, 119, 120, 265, 583*, colorplate 67]. *See* FRONTAL, VIEWPOINT. **2.** A portrait showing the sitter's head and shoulders as seen from the side; this usually lends the sitter an air of nobility and a measure of eternity not attainable in the more accidental and ephemeral three-quarter view [*187, 589*]. **3.** In architecture, the cross-section of a *molding*. Profiles were of intense concern to Gothic and Renaissance architects, as evidenced by the many carefully measured drawings of them that survive. Much of the apparent weightlessness of Gothic architecture results from the deeply grooved profiles of *ribs* and *tracery* which break up all masses into slender lines and edges [fig. 52, *367, 377, 383*].

PROGRAM. 1. In complex works of painting or sculpture, such as the Sistine Ceiling [*538*] or the portals of Chartres Cathedral [*396*], the underlying conceptual scheme—theological, humanistic, political, or personal—determining the choice of *subject* matter and symbolism. **2.** In architecture, all the requirements for a project, including use, materials and appearance, drawn up before construction begins. When a program exists in writing, or can be inferred historically with some accuracy, it provides an important basis for criticizing the effectiveness or success of the project and can be used to ward off irrelevant criticism.

PRONAOS (pro-nay′os; Gk. *pro*, before, + *naos*). The entrance chamber preceding the *naos*, or sanctuary, of a Greek temple, having continuations of the walls of the naos for its sides and a colonnade in front [*137*].

PROPORTION. In any object, figure, or composition, the relation, or ratio, of one part to another and of each part to the whole in regard to size, height, width, length, or depth. The proportions of an object are usually considered in relation to those of other objects of its kind or in relation to the normal proportions of the human body. A *column*, a man, or a statue of a man is called tall, short, thick, or thin in respect to its deviation from an established norm, or "canon," of proportion. The canon is usually based on a unit of measure called the *module*. The module most frequently taken to determine the proportions of the human body, for example, is the head, the normal human body being 7 or 7 $\frac{1}{2}$ "heads" tall. In determining the proportions of a classical column, the module taken is usually its diameter (or sometimes half of its diameter) measured at its base [fig. 29]; the slender Corinthian column may be 10 diameters high, but a column of the Greek Doric *order* may be 6$\frac{1}{2}$ or only 4 diameters. Thus, when the Greek Doric order was revived during the eighteenth century, at a time when the Corinthian was the most common order, it appeared remarkably austere and vigorous to those who liked the effect, but crude and squat to those who did not [cf. *682, 685*]. During the Romanesque and Gothic periods, the classical canons of proportion were often completely abandoned. Although the traditional division into base, shaft, and *capital* was retained, slender shafts, which to the classical eye appear as thin as sticks, sometimes sweep straight up from the pavements of churches to the ribs of the vaults [*335, 341, 369*]. Deviations from normal proportions are often found in the works of artists who, like the German

Expressionists, were concerned with portraying powerful emotional states; certain parts of the body, which may be emotionally significant, are enlarged or the body as a whole may be compressed or attenuated [*767, 769, 774–776,* colorplate 73; cf. *31, 32, 267, 326, 351–355, 361, 363,* colorplates 19, 45, *408, 548*]. Other artists, concerned with creating figures of unearthly beauty, grace, or elegance will also deviate from the norm, often establishing their own peculiar system of proportion [*64, 65, 174, 286, 288, 426,* colorplates 43, 60, *566–568, 838, 839*].

PSALTER (sawl'ter). A book containing the Psalms of the Bible. Many Psalters, richly *illuminated* with pictures illustrating literally the poetic imagery of the Psalms, have survived from the Middle Ages; the most famous is the Psalter in the library at the University of Utrecht [*327*].

PYLON (pai'lon; Gk., gateway). **1.** In Egyptian architecture, the monu-

Fig. 39. Perspective section of the Temple of Khonsu at Karnak (Chipiez): (a) sanctuary, (b) hypostyle hall, (c) forecourt, (d) pylon.

mental gateway to the forecourt of a temple, having in its developed form battered (sloping) walls edged with roll *moldings* and divided at the top into twin towers capped with large cavetto moldings [fig. 39, *60*]. **2.** Each one of the towers of such a gateway.

QIBLA (kib'la; Arabic). The direction faced by Moslems when praying, the direction of Mecca. The center of the "qibla wall" of a mosque is marked by a niche called the *mihrab*.

QUATREFOIL (kat'ruh-foyl; F. *quatre,* four, + *foil,* leaf). An ornamental figure composed of four lobes or foils [*403, 405, 419*]. A trefoil (tree'foyl *or* treh'foyl) has three foils [*432, 447*]. Both are common *motifs* in Gothic decoration and sometimes were intended as symbols, the trefoil referring to the Trinity and the quatrefoil to the Four Evangelists.

READY-MADE. A mass-produced utilitarian object which is transformed into a work of art simply by being placed in an artistic context or by being looked at as though it *were* a work of art. Marcel Duchamp was the first to demonstrate the principle of the ready-made by exhibiting a bottle-rack and a urinal. Any accidentally encountered object, mass-produced or not, is known as a "found object." or *objet trouvé* (oh-zhay troo-vay; F.). If it has been altered in any way, it is known as a "Found Object Assisted" and if two or more found objects are put together, the work so contrived is called an "assemblage" [*1*].

RED-FIGURED. A term applied to a type of Greek vase painting in which the figures were first outlined in black and the background then painted in with solid black, leaving the figures the reddish color of the baked clay after firing [*121, 122, 167*]. The red-figured style replaced the *black-figured* style toward the end of the sixth century B.C., probably because of the greater flexibility afforded by drawing with the brush rather than with the incising needle required for internal details in black-figure.

REFECTORY (re-fek'toree). The dining hall of a *monastery*, sometimes decorated with a representation of the *Last Supper* [fig. 28, *499, 524*].

REGISTER. One of a series of horizontal bands, placed one above the other, in a carved or painted decoration, as on the walls of an Egyptian tomb or on a Greek vase [*42, 74, 83, 90, 116, 263*].

REGULA (reg'yuh-la; *pl.* regulae; reg'yuh-lee; L., a straight-edge, rule). In an *entablature* of the Doric *order*, one of the series of short, projecting bands with *guttae*, placed beneath the *taenia*, just under each *triglyph* [*138, 139, 143, 146*]. Regulae should not be confused with *mutules*, the flat blocks with guttae beneath the Doric *cornice*.

RELIEF SCULPTURE. Sculpture which is not freestanding, but is carved or cast so that it projects from a surface of which it is part. The degree of projection is described as high (It. *alto rilievo*; ahl'toh ree-lyeh'voh), medium (It. *mezzo rilievo*), or low (It. *basso rilievo*; Fr. *bas-relief*; bah'ree-leef), high relief being almost detached from the surface and low relief being only slightly raised. Low relief was very widely used by the ancient Egyptians [*41, 43, 62, 66*], but they also used "sunken relief" which is much the same as ordinary relief sculpture except that the stone around the carving has not been cut back to form a background plane; instead, the highest points of the carving are on a level with the surface into which the carving has been cut [*63*]. Sunken relief not only saved the Egyptian sculptors the trouble of cutting away the stone to form a background plane, but it is a particularly effective form of exterior decoration in the bright sunlight of Egypt: the sharp edges surrounding the relief brilliantly catch the light on one side and cast a deep shadow on the opposite side, making the outlines of the figures visible at a great distance. During the fifteenth century, an extremely delicate form of low relief, called "rilievo schiacciato" (skyah-chyah'toh; It. flattened, crushed) was introduced by Donatello [474, 475]. With the slightest undulations of the surface, Donatello was able to catch and modulate the light in such a way as to achieve atmospheric effects which had hardly even been achieved in painting before his time.

RESPOND. A half-column, *pilaster*, or shaft projecting from a wall to support an *arch, rib, entablature*, etc., "in response" to a supporting member opposite, as in the wall at the end of an arcade or colonnade [*270*, colorplates 13, 31, *391*]. The shafts attached to, and rising from, the *compound piers* used in medieval churches, although they may not strictly be considered part of a wall, are sometimes called responds [fig. 52, *341, 342, 344, 373, 374*], as are the pilasters on a wall behind a colonnade [*218, 241, 485, 486, 529, 659*].

RHYTHM. In the visual arts, the regular repetition of a form. Rhythm varies according to the interval between repetitions, so one may speak of quick, moderate, measured, and slow rhythms. To a certain degree, the terms used to describe musical rhythms (allegro, presto, andante, largo, etc.) may be helpful in describing works of the visual arts as well, but it is important to realize that music is a temporal art and its terms cannot always be adequately applied to those effects in the visual arts which are largely spatial. If the columns of a colonnade are closely spaced, for example, they do not suggest quick movement to the viewer, but, instead, present a static barrier, even when the colonnade is seen frontally, but especially when it is seen at an angle; on the other hand, if columns are very widely spaced, the viewer may not relate them to each other at all. Some of the ways in which simple rhythms may be enriched are by varying the intervals between the units [fig. 43, *120, 271, 520, 577, 594*, colorplates 55, 61, 67, 70, *808, 813*], by contrasting a quick sequence with a slower one in a kind of visual counterpoint [*206, 336*, colorplate 32, *633, 809*], by introducing dissimilar units between similar units [*92, 263, 571, 572*, colorplate 58], or by intermixing one set of similar units with another set of units so that the different units alternate with each other [*198, 208, 227, 252, 293, 368*, colorplates 13, 20, 21, *545, 693*]. Rhythmic patterns are sometimes conveniently described by assigning letters of the alphabet to each unit, as in outlining the rhyme scheme of a poem. Thus, a simple repetition of a single unit might be indicated as AAAA. . . , an alternating pattern as ABABA, etc. A very common pattern in architecture is the ABA pattern used, for example, on the Arch of Constantine [*241*] and imitated by Alberti at S. Andrea in Mantua [*503*]. The undulating rhythms of continuous lines and outlines [*88, 103, 113, 182, 316, 355*, colorplates 68, 79] are less precisely designated, but are often more suggestive of movement than the rhythm of detached units.

RHYTON (rai'tahn; Gk. fr. *rhytos*, flowing). An ancient drinking horn, often shaped like the head or body of an animal [*93, 108*].

RIB. A slender arched support such as those projecting from the surfaces of Romanesque and Gothic *vaults*. Transverse ribs were often used to stiffen the tunnel vaults of Romanesque churches [*333, 335*] and, in a few later Romanesque churches with cross-vaults, diagonal ribs along the groins were also used [*340–342, 344*]; this became customary in Gothic architecture [fig. 52, *369, 370, 373, 374, 380, 381*]. In Early and High Gothic architecture, the analogy with the ribs of the human body is particularly appropriate since the masonry ribs form a delicate framework which supports the thin web of the vaults. The ribs were apparently erected first and then a portable "centering" (wooden support) was hung from them to hold the web of each section of the vault until the mortar dried. In much of later Gothic architecture, however, the ribbing, often very elaborate, is largely ornamental rather than structural [*382*].

ROSE WINDOW. A great circular window with an elaborate pattern of *tracery* and stained glass, frequently found on the façades and at the ends of the *transepts* of Gothic churches [*371–373, 375, 392*].

ROSETTE (ro-zet′). Any ornament resembling a flower and approximately circular in shape [fig. 26, right; *100, 117, 293, 318*].

RUSTICATION. The method of cutting and laying up masonry so that the

Fig. 40. Sixteenth-century project for a rusticated gateway (Delorme).

joints are deeply recessed. This reveals the mass of each block and gives the wall an appearance of great strength, especially appropriate for the base or ground floor of a building [*660*]. The blocks may be either smooth-faced with beveled edges [*501, 674*] or rough-hewn [*394, 809*]. In the Palazzo Medici in Florence [*491*], the different types are clearly juxtaposed: rough-hewn rustication is used for the ground floor, smooth-faced rustication for the second, and unrusticated "ashlar" (blocks of smooth-faced stone laid up evenly with fine joints) for the top story. Rustication was so admired during the sixteenth century that even columns were bound by rough-hewn segments and projecting bands, conveying a sense of unresolved conflict between the smooth, obviously man-made members and the rough, apparently natural, segments [fig. 40, *572*, colorplate 50].

SACRISTY (sak′ris-tee). A room in a church, usually near the main altar, where the sacred vessels and vestments used in the performance of the services are kept.

SALON (sah-lon′[nasal]; F. fr. It. *salone*). **1.** A reception room in a large French house [*670*]. In Germany, such a room [colorplate 58] is called a "Saal" (zahl). **2.** An art exhibition, such as the great exhibition held annually at Paris since the mid-eighteenth century. Many of the large carefully prepared paintings by Géricault [*717, 718*], Delacroix [*720*], and Courbet [*736*]—so huge that they are sometimes called salon "machines"—were painted for these great public exhibitions.

SANGUINE (sang′gwin; fr. L. *sanguis*, blood). A reddish-brown chalk frequently used by Renaissance and Baroque artists for drawing [*556*].

SARCOPHAGUS (sar-kof′a-gus; *pl.* sarcophagi; sar-kof′a-jai). A large, and often impressively ornamented, stone coffin [*190, 263, 541*].

SATURATION. That property of a color by which its vividness or purity is distinguished; also called "intensity" or "chroma." A color may have the same *hue* or *value* as another, but differ from it in saturation; the more vivid of two such colors is said to be of "higher saturation;" the less distinct of the two, which may be so neutral that its hue is hardly discernible, is said to be of "low saturation." The purity and amount of *pigment* applied to a given area will affect its degree of saturation, but the different hues, by the nature of their pigments, are normally higher or lower in saturation at one level of value than at another. Red-orange and green-blue, for example, are most highly saturated at a medium level of value and lose their saturation if their values are raised or lowered [colorplates 52, 62]. Yellow, however, is highly saturated only when it is high in value [colorplates 53, 62] and violet, when it is low in value. The relative level of value at which each hue reaches its highest saturation is indicated in the following diagram:

By using highly saturated violets in shadows, Turner and the Impressionists were able to increase the intensity of their paintings without upsetting the usual scale of values; their shadows could be both dark *and* intense. This can be seen by squinting at one of their paintings or good color reproductions of them, because squinting reduces the effect of hue and saturation and emphasizes value contrasts. Colors which are highly saturated and insistent when the eyes are wide open will be reduced largely to value alone when one squints. It will then be seen that the insistence or prominence of colors like violet is due to their high saturation, not their value level; they may, indeed, be very dark [colorplates 63, 67, 69, 71, 74]. The relative insistence of highly saturated colors at various levels of value can also be gauged by comparing accurate black-and-white reproductions with accurate color reproductions of the same painting [cf. colorplate 26 and *443*, colorplate 28 and *444*, colorplate 32 and *498*, colorplate 55 and *669*]. The highly saturated yellows, since they are most intense at high values, remain insistent when reduced solely to value in black and white reproductions, but the reds, blues, and violets lose much of their distinctness when reduced to dull grays and blacks.

SCALE (fr. L. *scala*, ladder, staircase). **1.** Any graduated series, as a "scale of *values* from white to black." **2.** A measuring strip on a *plan, elevation*, map, etc., indicating the precise degree to which all parts have been reduced in size so that their true dimensions can be quickly determined [*69, 142, 145*]. **3.** The relative size of an object, usually considered in relation to other objects of its kind or to the size of a man. When certain figures in a painting or relief are presented as larger in scale than others because of their importance in a social or religious hierarchy, the device is known as "hierarchic scaling" [*42, 55, 67, 76, 353, 412, 426, 452, 579, 786, 843*]. Relative importance within a general system of values also accounts for the exaggerated or diminished scale of some classes of inanimate objects [*83, 120, 233*, colorplate 12, *428*]. Certain parts of the body, too, may be represented on a larger scale than others, because of their special expressive significance [*16, 31, 73, 130, 287, 326, 361*, colorplate 19, *775, 784*]. In architectural design, more purely visual or structural reasons usually account for the appearance of the same *motif* at different scales [*212, 281, 282, 303, 306, 338, 503, 577, 685*]. Architecture is said to lack "human scale" when its parts are not clearly related to the normal size of a man. Some parts of a building must be of a familiar size or its true dimensions cannot be grasped [*391, 608*]. **4.** The apparent size of an object regardless of its absolute or precisely measurable size. Some objects are very small in size but large in scale [*16, 113, 118, 183, 185, 186, 847*]; others are very large in size, but surprisingly small in scale [*130, 420, 426, 720, 732, 735*]. In studying works of art from small reproductions it is always necessary to note their true dimensions before one can gain any idea of the full effect of the original. *See* MONUMENTAL.

SCRIPTORIUM (skrip-toh′ree-um; *pl.* scriptoria, fr. L. *scribere, scriptum*, to write, + *-orium*, place for). The workroom in a *monastery* where manuscripts were copied and *illuminated*.

SCULPTURE. *See* CASTING, KINETIC SCULPTURE, MOBILE, MODELING, READY-MADE, RELIEF SCULPTURE, TERRACOTTA.

SECONDARY COLORS. The hues resulting from the mixture of two *primary colors*. The secondaries are orange (red + yellow), green (blue + yellow), and violet (blue + red). In the "color wheel" in fig. 11, each shaded circle is a secondary, obtained by mixing the primaries to either side of it.

SECTION. A representation of a building, object or site showing it as it would appear if it were cut open along a plane passing through it vertically [*49, 107, 257*]. A "longitudinal section" shows the building as though it had been cut lengthwise [*272*] and a "transverse section," or "cross-section," shows it as though it had been cut crosswise. Most sections are made to *scale* so that all vertical dimensions can be measured accurately, but horizontal dimensions, which are not parallel to the picture plane, are *foreshortened*. A "perspective section" [*617*], while gaining in pictorial effect, is directly measurable only at the plane of the cut. *See* ELEVATION, PLAN.

SFUMATO (sfoo-mah'toh; It., vanished, gone up in smoke). The very subtle gradations of light and dark developed by Leonardo to *model* his figures. Leonardo's *sfumato* lends a sensuous softness and, at times, a tantalizing ambiguity to his forms, as in the famous smile of the *Mona Lisa* [*522–524, 526*; cf. *549, 557*]. The use of *sfumato* in the mythologies of Correggio, however, is frankly voluptuous [*563*]. *See* CHIAROSCURO, TONE, VALUE.

SHADE. An old and convenient term still used to designate a color mixed with black. Since black lowers the *value* of the basic color (i.e., darkens it), shades were frequently used to model forms before the advent of color *modeling* with the Impressionists. When a color is mixed with white it is called a *tint*. Hogarth makes this distinction between shades and tints in his book *The Analysis of Beauty* (1753), but the terms are still generally used as synonymns for "color" or to describe any variation of color.

SHADING. In drawing, painting, or printmaking, the darkening of parts of an object and its surroundings to suggest the effect of light falling upon it. In drawings and prints this may be done by *hatching* and in paintings, by using *shades* of the "local color," or basic *hue*, of the object. *See* HIGHLIGHTS, MODELING, SHADOW.

SHADOW. In painting, drawing, and printmaking, a darkened portion of a picture representing areas of the subject cut off from direct illumination. A "cast shadow" is a shadow of more or less definite shape formed on a surface behind a body that blocks the light. The strong spatial effect created solely by a cast shadow is demonstrated in fig. 41. This effect can be seen in Manet's

Fifer [Louvre, colorplate 64]. This is a remarkably flat, shadowless painting for its period, but if the cast shadows (beneath the right foot and behind the left leg) and the shadows at the top and bottom of the canvas are covered, it will look even flatter. Cast shadows first appear in Hellenistic and Roman painting [*243, 245, 247, 249*], but they were not represented again until the early fifteenth century [colorplate 25]. The Master of Flémalle carefully reproduced the double cast shadows

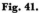
Fig. 41.

created by two different sources of light falling on the same object [colorplate 28] and Jan van Eyck regularly distinguished between the darker central portion of cast shadows, called the "umbra," and the lighter periphery, the "penumbra" [*446, 447, 449, 450*]. The Venetian painters of the sixteenth century and many Baroque masters used shadows more arbitrarily; by veiling the less important parts of their compositions in shadow, they gave dramatic emphasis to the figures in the light [colorplates 41, 49].

SHAPE. A shape is formed whenever a line turns or lines meet, even though an area may not be entirely enclosed. Thus, we speak of C-shapes, S-shapes, T-shapes, X-shapes, etc. The shape of a three-dimensional form is determined by its outline or silhouette. A shape need not be entirely delineated before it becomes distinctly recognizable; it may only be implied. Figs. 42 and 43, for example, show triangular and oval shapes implied on the *picture planes* of paintings by the arrangement of the heads of figures; both of these configurations have a directional character because they have been extended in one direction more than another: the triangle points upward and the oval is formed along a dynamic oblique *axis*. Repetitions of shapes, all pointing in the same direction, can give a composition a powerful directional character as in the sweeping vertical shafts, *buttresses*, *pinnacles* and towers of a Gothic church [fig. 52, *374, 375, 377, 393*]. Fig. 44 shows the upward-pointing shapes in the famous mosaic of the Emperor Justinian at San Vitale in Ravenna [cf. *271*]; a similar diagram might be made of the downward-pointing shapes as well. Sometimes the harmony attained by variations of a basic shape, or by repetition of the smaller shapes within a work, is the chief means by which an artist builds his composition [*16, 35, 120, 312,* colorplates 67, 72, 77, 79, *797, 802, 808, 829, 833, 846*]; this is especially true of

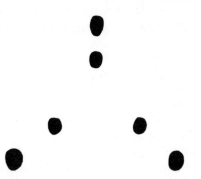

Fig. 42. Implied shape formed by heads in Masaccio's "Trinity."

Fig. 43. Implied shape formed by heads in Poussin's "Rape of the Sabine Women."

Fig. 44.

architecture [*212, 276, 282, 297–306, 395, 531, 577, 813–828, 849*]. *See*
COMPOSITION, CONTOUR, FIGURE-GROUND RELATIONSHIP.

SIDE AISLE. One of the corridors running parallel to the *nave* of a church
and separated from it by an arcade or colonnade [figs. 10, 52, *253, 254*].

SINOPIA (see-noh′pee-a; *pl.* sinopie; see-noh′pee-ay; It., fr. Sinope, a city in
Asia Minor famous for its red earth pigment). **1.** A reddish-brown earth color.
2. In *fresco* painting, a full-scale drawing, usually red, made on the rough
plaster of a wall to establish the main parts of a composition before the final
coat of plaster is applied for painting [*436*].

SKELETAL CONSTRUCTION. A form of construction in which the weight-
bearing members are reduced to a slender framework, walls and windows
being no more than thin membranes either hung from the structural skeleton
or supporting only themselves as in Gothic churches [fig. 52, *374, 376, 382*]
and twentieth-century buildings with a frame of steel or *ferroconcrete* [*810–
812, 818–825*; cf. *806*].

SPAN. The distance between the members supporting a *lintel, arch, truss, vault,*
etc. [fig.1].

STALACTITES. Tiny pendant arches used as an ornament in Moslem
architecture; they resemble the natural stalactites hanging like icicles from
the ceilings of caverns [*300*].

STELE (stee′lee; Gk., standing rock). An upright slab carved with commemorative reliefs or inscriptions [*76, 79, 165*].

STEREOBATE. A solid mass of masonry serving as the visible base of a
building, especially a Greek temple [*138*]. In the crepidoma (kreh-pee-
doh′ma), or stepped base, of a Greek temple, only the lower steps are called
the stereobate; the top step, on which the columns rest, is called the stylobate
(sty′lo-bayt).

STEREOMETRIC (fr. Gk. *stereos*, solid, + *metron*, measure). Pertaining to
stereometry, the science of measuring solids and the art of cutting stones
into geometrical forms, as for Gothic *vaulting* and *tracery* [fig. 52, *367, 369*].
The figures painted by such Renaissance perspectivists as Piero della Fran-
cesca [colorplate 32, *498*] and Paolo Uccello [colorplate 33] are sometimes
described as stereometric because of their apparent solidity and their geometrical clarity and simplicity.

STUPA (stoo′pa; Sanskrit). A Buddhist reliquary mound. The Great Stupa
at Sanchi in India [*839*] is a solid *dome* on a *drum*; there is a narrow walkway
around the base of the dome and the whole mound is surrounded by a
circular stone railing with tall gateways at north, east, south, and west.

STYLE. The distinctive and characteristic way of making and arranging the
forms of a work of art by which it may be assigned to a particular period,
place, artist or period within an artist's life. *See* HAND, HANDLING.

STYLOBATE. *See* STEREOBATE.

SUBJECT. In the representational arts, that which is represented, as distinguished from the particular form and expressive content of any single represen-

tation of it. *See* ANDACHTSBILD, FÊTE GALANTE, GENRE, ODALISQUE, PROGRAM. The subject of a work of art is usually determined before work is begun. However, if a specific subject has not been commissioned by a patron or if the artist is not working directly from nature, the subject may change as he works or emerge only gradually in the process of working with purely abstract forms. This is particularly true of twentieth-century painting and sculpture. Although an artist may occasionally attempt a strikingly original subject, the general subject-matter of a work of art is usually traditional and has been treated many times before. Even if an artist deliberately sets out to copy another work, however, his version will be distinguished from all others by his own personal *handling* of the forms and the way in which they have been organized [cf. *5* and *6, 7* and *10*]. With the alteration of form there will be a concomitant change in the expressive effect of the work on the viewer. Sometimes the expressive effect of the work (as distinguished from both its subject and its form) is called its "content." Subject, form, and content, however, are necessarily interrelated and can only be separated for purposes of analysis. Examples of some of the ways in which they are related in a version of a particular subject are given in the entry for COMPOSITION.

SUN-BREAK (fr. F. *brise-soleil*; breez so-lay′). A screen of large horizontal or vertical fins projecting from the walls of a building to shade the windows. Le Corbusier was the first to use the device on a large scale [*825*].

SUPERIMPOSED ORDERS. *Orders* placed one above the other on the face of a building of more than one story [*208, 218, 501, 505, 572, 663, 674*]. Superimposition of the orders is also known simply as "superposition" or "supercolumniation." When different orders are used, the stoutest is placed at the bottom and the most slender at the top.

SYMMETRY. Balance achieved by correspondence of parts on either side of a central *axis*. The corresponding parts may be identical or, when irregular shapes are used, one side may be reversed, as in a mirror image [figs. 10, 35, *16, 27, 40, 42, 61, 82, 88, 111, 124, 259, 308, 313, 318*]. In either case, the term "bilateral symmetry" is sometimes used to stress the extreme regularity of the arrangement. In the composition of figure groups, figures on one side of a central vertical axis are sometimes given the same postures as those on the other side, but, to insure the symmetry of the group, their outlines may have to be reversed by representing them as though seen from the other side or from behind [*131, 134, 551*]. There may be some degree of variation to either side of the axis, but as long as a group is arranged about a dominant central axis and there is a considerable degree of correspondence between forms on both sides, the arrangement may be called symmetrical [*230, 264, 284, 288, 291, 396*, colorplate 24, *518, 520, 524, 550*]. Symmetry almost completely dominated monumental architecture until the nineteenth century, but painters and sculptors, as a rule, have had a strong aversion to it ever since the beginning of the seventeenth century. *See* BALANCE.

TABLINUM (ta-bly′num; L. fr. *tabula*, record, writing tablet). In a Roman house, a recess or chamber, usually at the far end of the *atrium*, where family records and portraits were kept [fig. 19, *216*].

TACTILE (fr. L. *tactus*, touch). Pertaining to the sense of touch. The "tactile values," which the *connoisseur* Bernhard Berenson thought were the essence of Renaissance painting, refer to the impression of three-dimensional relief and apparent tangibility created by painters on the two-dimensional surfaces of their pictures. In describing works of art, "tactile" is sometimes used as a synonym for "plastic." *See* PLASTICITY.

TAENIA (tee'nee-a; L., fillet or headband). In an *entablature* of the Doric *order*, the thin, flat *molding* running beneath the *triglyphs* and separating the *architrave* from the *frieze* [fig. 29, *138, 139, 146*].

TEMPERA. Pigments mixed, or "tempered," with any of a number of water soluble media—including egg, glue, and casein (milk)—which leave a matte surface when dry. A bright and very durable tempera, made with egg yolk, was widely used for panel painting by fourteenth- and fifteenth-century Italian artists and it is generally egg tempera which is meant when the word "tempera" alone is used by art historians and *connoisseurs* [colorplates 23–26]. Since tempera drys very quickly and does not blend easily, the paint was usually applied in a fine *hatching* of short strokes which allow lower layers of color, such as the green *underpainting* customary during the fourteenth century, to show through the spaces between them. Tempera, unlike *oil paint* or *watercolor*, is an opaque medium encouraging clear, sharp outlines and does not permit the use of transparent *washes* and *glazes*. To relieve the dry effect of pure tempera painting, many fifteenth- and sixteenth-century painters employed a "mixed method," superimposing oil glazes over a tempera underpainting, thereby uniting the precision of tempera with the luminosity of oil.

TERRACOTTA (It., baked earth). **1.** Fired clay, modeled, or molded, and baked until it is very hard. Terracotta has been used since ancient times for pottery and sculpture and as a building material. It may be coated with a *glaze* of molten glass [*508, 812*], painted [*190, 195*], or left untreated after firing [*665, 671*]; after the first firing, but before glazing, it is sometimes called "biscuit" or "bisque" because of its porousness. **2.** An object made of terracotta. **3.** A color resembling the brownish red hue of terracotta.

TESSERAE (tess'er-ee; *sing.* tessera; L.). The small squares of stone or glass used in making a *mosaic* [colorplates 14, 15].

THERMAE (thur'mee; L., hot baths, fr. Gk. *therme*, heat). One of the great Roman public baths, which besides providing various rooms for bathing and swimming (a "tepidarium" or warm room, a "caldarium" or hot room, a "frigidarium" or cool room, etc.) was also equipped with almost all the conveniences of a modern social and athletic club.

THOLOS (thoh'los; *pl.* tholoi; Gk.). In Greek and Roman architecture, a circular building [*151, 201*].

THRUST. The downward and outward pressure exerted by an *arch* or *vault*, resulting from the pull of gravity on its members. Within the arch or vault itself, thrust is strongest at the haunches and if the arch or vault is not loaded or abutted at these critical points [fig. 3], it may collapse. Every vault or roof *truss*, as a whole, also exerts thrust against the walls supporting it;

unless the walls are thick enough to contain this thrust, *buttresses* must be set against the wall at those points where the pressure is greatest [figs. 10, 52, *334, 385*].

TINT. Loosely, a synonym for "color," but more specifically a color obtained by mixing a basic *hue* with white to raise its *value*, i.e. to lighten it. Tints are frequently used for *highlights* in *modeling*. *Cf.* SHADE.

TONE. Loosely, any color, but more specifically a *value* or *shade*. During the sixteenth and seventeenth centuries, tonal painting, in which an entire composition is treated in broad areas of light and dark, largely replaced the bright and even hues and the regular *modeling* favored by artists of the Early Renaissance [cf. colorplates 31–38 with 39–41, 49–57, 61, 62]. *See* CHIARO-SCURO, SFUMATO.

TRACERY. In Gothic architecture, the ornamental stonework carved in geometrical patterns, originally in the upper part of pointed windows, but then applied to almost any surface in any medium [fig. 52, *378*]. In the ear-liest form of tracery, called "plate tracery," the glass appears to have been inserted into holes punched into solid stone, as at Chartres Cathedral [*373*, colorplate 21]. In the later "bar tracery," the glass predominates over the slender stone bars, which flow from the vertical "mullions" dividing each window into "lights" [*376*]. In Flamboyant Gothic, which takes its name from the flame-like patterns of the tracery of later Gothic churches, the bars flow in restlessly undulating curves [*377, 463, 464*].

TRANSEPT (fr. L. *trans*, across, + *septum*, an enclosure). In a cruciform church, the whole arm set at right angles to the *nave*. The separate projec-tions on either side of the nave, which constitute the transept as a whole, are distinguished as the "north transept" and the "south transept." The area of the transept which intersects the nave is called the *crossing* [fig. 10].

TREFOIL. *See* QUATREFOIL.

TRIFORIUM (try-for'ee-um; *pl.* triforia). In a church without a gallery, the arcaded level of the *nave* wall between the great nave arcade and the *clerestory* [fig. 52]. In some Early Gothic churches which have galleries, the triforium lies between the gallery and the clerestory to form a four-story elevation. Since it is usually at the level of the lean-to roofs over the *side aisles*, the triforium arcade may be *blind* [*336*] or have only a narrow pas-sageway set behind it [colorplate 21]. In some High Gothic churches, in which the roofs of the side aisles and the *ambulatory* are free of the triforium, the triforium, as well as the clerestory, is glazed [*374*].

TRIGLYPH (try'glif; fr. Gk. *tri*, three, + *glyphe*, carved work). In the *frieze* of the *entablature* of the Doric *order*, the vertical blocks which are divided by channels into three sections. Originally, in wooden construction, the triglyphs were probably the ends of ceiling beams [fig. 29, *138, 139, 143, 144, 529, 684, 685*].

TRIPTYCH (trip'tik). An *altarpiece* of three panels, usually hinged so that the outer "wings" or "shutters" cover the larger central panel when closed [*290, 432, 444, 452, 455*]. *Cf.* DIPTYCH.

TROPHY. An ornament composed of the instruments and spoils of war—arms, armor, standards, and drums—heaped up like the victory memorials of antiquity [*516, 660, 677*].

TRUMEAU (troo-moh; *pl.* trumeaux, F.). A *pillar* placed in the center of a large doorway to support the *lintel* [fig. 45]. The trumeaux of medieval church portals frequently bear figures or statues [*351, 405, 409*].

Fig. 45. South Portal, S. Pierre, Moissac.

TRUSS. A framework of wood or metal composed of members fastened to form rigid triangles [fig. 46]. Timber trusses were used in roofing many medieval and Early Renaissance churches; in these, the trusses may be left exposed [*253, 387*] or covered with a flat wooden ceiling, which is often *coffered* [*331, 348, 485*].

Fig. 46. Sixteenth-century design for a roof truss (Serlio).

TYMPANUM (tim'pa-num; *pl.* tympana; fr. L., drum). **1.** In classical architecture, the recessed face of a *pediment*. **2.** In medieval architecture, the surface enclosed by the arch and *lintel* of an arched doorway, frequently carved with *relief sculpture* [fig. 45, *354, 396, 399*].

UNDERPAINTING. The preparatory painting, in line and broad *washes*, applied directly to the gesso (jess'oh; plaster of Paris) ground of a canvas or panel to establish the main *contours* and *values*. In Italy, during the fourteenth century, green was usually used, but, from the fifteenth century on, a warm brown monochrome became customary. The brown underpainting, often quite dark, was then largely covered over with opaque layers of paint or semi-transparent *glazes* which allowed parts of the underpainting to show through. Sometimes, because of the tendency of the upper layers of paint to become transparent with age, the underpainting shows through in spots, and, although this spoils the effect intended by the artist, it may have much to tell us about his method of working and about his original intentions, which may change as the work progresses. "Pentimenti" (It., regrets)— parts that were altered by overpainting—for example, often show up and sometimes indicate, not only corrections, but significant changes in subject-matter. In some cases, the underpainting can be examined directly, because the work was never finished [*522*], or it can be studied through X-ray photographs. Since the nineteenth century, however, the "alla prima" technique (al'la pree'ma; It., at once)—painting without any preparatory drawing or painting—has become cutomary. *See* SINOPIA.

VALUE. That property of a color by which it is distinguished as light or dark, as in the distinction between "light green" and "dark green" or "light blue" and "dark blue." The values of colors—and only their values— are seen in black-and-white reproductions of paintings; the other properties of the colors, their *hue* and *saturation*, are not reproduced [cf. colorplates 28, 32, 45, 55 with their corresponding black-and-white reproductions, *444, 498, 560, 669*]. Value is the sole distinguishing feature of the "achro-matic" colors—white, black, and the range of grays between them; they do not have the additional properties of hue and saturation shared by the "chromatic" colors. Therefore, reproductions of achromatic prints and drawing are likely to be more accurate than even color reproductions of paintings because of the fewer factors involved and the consequently smaller margin of error.

Colors which are light are said to be "high" in value; those that are dark are said to be "low" in value. Colors may be raised in value by mixing with white to make a *tint* or lowered in value by mixing with black to make a *shade*. Tints and shades of a basic color are often used in *modeling*, but the addition of the white or black pigment usually weakens the effect of hue and saturation. Since only effects of light and dark can be rendered when working in black and white, artists sometimes raise or lower the normal values of objects, or parts of objects, represented in their drawings to compensate for the loss of contrast resulting from the elimination of hue and saturation. Drawings in which this is done systematically are called "color value" drawings. Sometimes, as in the "spotlighting" used by Rembrandt [*635, 636, 639*], the lights and darks in pictures are "crowded" toward the ex-tremes of the value scale and the middle values are reduced. This increases dramatic effect and emphasizes the parts in the light. Crowding of the lights and darks is especially characteristic of sixteenth-century Venetian painting and much Baroque painting [colorplates 40, 41, 44, 49, *555, 564, 613, 642,*

649, 651]. In many of these pictures, edges are often lightened where dark shapes lie against dark grounds and darkened when light shapes lie against light grounds, thereby snapping the shapes forward by increasing the separation of *figure and ground* [colorplates 45, 52, *559, 561, 627*]. *See* CHIAROSCURO, SFUMATO, TONE.

VANISHING POINT. In pictures constructed according to the principles of linear *perspective*, the point or points of convergence for all lines forming an angle with the *picture plane*. In single-point perspective, all "orthogonals" (lines which are perpendicular to the picture plane) [fig. 36] converge toward a vanishing point lying directly opposite the eye of the observer, at the level of the horizon [fig. 30a]. In two-point perspective, in which objects are placed at an angle other than a right angle with the picture plane, the vanishing points lie on the horizon to either side of the object drawn in perspective [fig. 47, *740*; cf. *502, 505*]. Their distance from the object depends on the distance of the viewer: if the viewer is near the object, the vanishing points will be close to the object and it will be sharply *foreshortened*; if the viewer is far from the object, the vanishing points will be farther away from it and may even lie outside the picture plane [cf. figs. 47a and 47b]. Three-point perspective was sometimes used in constructing *illusionistic* ceiling decorations [*625*, colorplate 58]; this is the same as two-point perspective with respect to the convergence of horizontal lines, but a third vanishing point is added to allow for the convergence of all vertical lines. To maintain a sense of structure and stability, however, this very natural and easily observed effect of convergence is usually ignored and

a

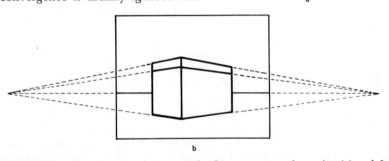

b

Fig. 47. Building drawn in two-point perspective from a near station point (a) and from a more distant station point (b).

all verticals are kept rigidly parallel to one another and to the sides of the picture, even when a low *viewpoint*, close to the object, is assumed [516]. *See* FOCAL POINT, PERSPECTIVE, VIEWPOINT.

VAULT. A ceiling or roof of brick, stone, or concrete built on the principle of the *arch*. A "tunnel vault," or "barrel vault," is a tunnel-like semi-cylindrical extension of an arch, which may be thought of as an unbroken series of arches pressed together, one behind the other [fig. 48]. It cannot be lighted except at the ends without being structurally weakened, because, as in an arch, continuous abutment must be applied to absorb the *thrust* carried down along the haunches to the walls supporting it [fig. 48; cf. fig. 3; *241, 301, 492, 516, 550*]. However, arches may be

Fig. 48.

Fig. 49.

introduced in the supporting walls [*212, 213, 256–258, 337, 608*] and transverse *ribs* may be inserted in the vault [*335*] to concentrate thrust at a few strongly *buttressed* points [*333, 334*], thereby permitting a reduction of weight and thrust in the segments of vaulting between the ribs. If a tunnel vault is intersected at right angles by another tunnel vault of the same size [fig. 49], a "cross-vault," or "groin vault," is formed [figs. 50, 51, *209*]. This is a very efficient form of vault allowing full illumination from the sides; thus, a series of groin vaults is often used at a high level to form a range of *clerestory* windows lighting a great hall [*213*] or *nave*. Groin vaults also allow a great saving in material and labor over the simple tunnel vault; thrust is concentrated along the "groins" (the four diagonal edges formed along the points where the tunnel vaults intersect), so the vault need only be

Fig. 50. Groin vault seen from below.

Fig. 51. Groin vault seen from above.

Fig. 52. Perspective section of nave bay of Amiens Cathedral (Viollet-le-Duc): (A) nave arcade, (B) triforium, (C) clerestory, (D) side aisle, (E) buttress, (F) pinnacle, (a) blind arcade, (b) compound pier, (c) respond, (d) mullion, (e) tracery, (f) transverse rib, (g) diagonal rib, (h) boss, (i) molding profile, (j) strut, (k) finial.

abutted at its four corners [*213*]. In some Romanesque churches [*341*] and most Gothic churches, the groins of the cross-vaults are ribbed. The use of diagonal *ribs* along the groins—together with wall ribs and transverse ribs at the four sides of the vault—radically changed the basic visual effect of vaulting from one of broadly curving surfaces to one of cellular division

Fig. 53. Semicircular ribs of a cross-vault raised over a square bay; the crowns of the ribs at the sides of the square are lower than the crowns of the diagonal ribs.

and linear movement [fig. 52; *367–370, 373, 374*]. The ribs reduced the quantity of centering (wooden supports) required during construction and permitted a thinner vault, reduced thrust, and therefore reduced mass throughout the building, allowing larger areas for stained-glass windows. The pointed arches used for the ribs of Gothic vaulting are more stable than

Fig. 54. Semicircular ribs of a cross-vault raised over an oblong bay; ribs of three different heights.

the semi-circular ribs used in Romanesque vaulting, because they are more nearly vertical. They also permit greater variety in planning without the awkward changes in the heights of ribs which occur when strictly semi-circular arches are used. When a vault with semi-circular ribs is raised over a square *bay*, for example, the crowns of the arches will be at two

Fig. 55. Pointed ribs of equal height raised over an oblong bay.

different levels, because the diagonal ribs must span a greater distance than the ribs at the sides of the square [fig. 53, *344*]. Over an oblong bay, the crowns will be at three different levels because there will be three different *spans* [fig. 54]. If pointed arches are used, however, the crowns can all be raised to the same height [fig. 55] without the obvious distortions of shape which occur when what one expects to be a semi-circular rib is depressed or has the level of its springing raised, or "stilted" [*341, 342*].

VELLUM (fr. Middle Fr. *veel*, calf). Calfskin prepared for writing or painting upon, a superior type of *parchment* widely used for medieval manuscripts.

VESTIBULE (ves'tih-byool). A hall or passage between the main entrance and the interior of a building [*542, 658*]. In the ancient Roman house, the "vestibulum" was a recess between the front door and the street [fig. 19].

VIEWPOINT. The point from which a viewer looks at an object or visual field. In an ordinary photograph or in a picture constructed according to the principles of linear *perspective*, everything is represented as seen from a single viewpoint; every object can be clearly located in relation to this viewpoint according to its position above or below it, to the left or right of it, and close to it or far from it [figs. 30, 47]. Thus the general position of the viewpoint assumed by an artist in making a picture can be quickly determined by observing which parts of the objects represented can be seen and which cannot: if the top of something is shown, the viewpoint must be located above it; if the bottom is shown, then it is seen from below, etc. Most pictures, however, are not systematically constructed and sometimes parts of a composition or parts of a single object may be represented as though seen from an entirely different viewpoint than others [*246, 428, 743, 756, 770, 789*]. When this is done as a matter of course, as in Egyptian painting or the pictures of Picasso in which a *frontal* eye may be placed in a head shown in *profile* or legs in profile attached to a frontal torso, the method is called "fractional representation" [*43, 55, 63*, colorplates 5, 75, *784*]. *See* FOCAL PIONT, KINETIC SCULPTURE, PERSPECTIVE, VANISHING POINT.

VOLUME. Any three-dimensional quantity bounded or enclosed, whether a solid or a void. Although "volume" is frequently used as a synonym for "mass," it is very useful, in analyzing works of art, to distinguish between solid volumes and hollow volumes, or "positive volumes" and "negative volumes." Many buildings, for example, appear from the outside to be a single solid volume, but on the inside may contain a spatial volume which is at least as impressive as the mass which bounds it [cf. *210* and *211*; *274* and *276*]. In Egyptian architecture and sculpture, solids usually predominate over voids [*48–52*], but in architecture and sculpture of the Gothic period and of the twentieth century, hollows are often more important than masses [*374, 377, 402, 462, 805, 806, 808, 822, 828*]. In classical and High Renaissance art there is usually a balance of solid volumes and hollow volumes [*143, 164, 177, 206–209, 529, 530, 534, 535*].

VOLUTE (vo-loot'; fr. L. *volutus*, rolled). An ornament resembling a rolled scroll, especially prominent on the *capitals* of the Ionic and Composite orders [fig. 29, *138, 150, 200, 256*]. Similar spirals, but smaller in size, curl out from the tops of Corinthian capitals as well [fig. 26, *149*]. In Renaissance and Baroque architecture, volutes were used on a large scale to link even such major units as the upper story of a church façade with the lower [*542, 577, 622, 663*].

VOUSSOIR (voo-swar; F.). One of the wedge-shaped stones used to construct an *arch* [figs. 1, 5].

WALL. Any very broad upright structure or surface serving as a barrier, enclosure or support. Walls may be free-standing and self-supporting, as a city-wall, parapet, or sacred enclosure [*46, 81, 111, 226, 294*]; they may be non-structural "screen-walls" or "curtain-walls" shielding the interior of a building against the weather and the noise of the outside world but permitting light to enter through glass windows as in the almost wall-less structure of a Gothic church or modern steel-frame office building [fig. 52, *367, 374 376, 382, 811, 818–825*]; inside a building they may be no more than space dividers [*687*]; or they may be thick structural "bearing walls" supporting a roof, a *vault*, or floor beams [*253, 322, 329, 336, 491, 547, 617, 809*].

WARM COLORS. The *hues* commonly associated with fire: reds, oranges, and yellows. Titian and Rubens are notable among painters who developed the color composition of their works with contrasting warm and *cool colors* [colorplates 41, 50]. Normally, warm colors appear to advance and cool colors to recede, a tendency exploited in color *modeling*. The color and quantity of illumination received by an object may alter this effect, however. Yellow, although very insistent under ordinary natural light, loses its insistency when the illumination falls off, whereas blue, a cool color, gains in insistence. This is very noticeable if, while looking at a painting or color reproduction in natural light, a cloud passes over the sun; the balance of the colors changes: the blues may suddenly appear to "jump out" and the yellows to recede relative to the blues. To demonstrate this to yourself, look at colorplates 59, 68, 73, and 77 in strong sunlight and then in a dark corner.

WASH. In painting, especially *watercolor*, and brush drawing, a broad, thin film of highly diluted pigment [*580, 656, 691*]. Washes are often used in overlapping layers to *model* forms, darker or more highly *saturated* areas being built up by several applications of a basic semi-transparent wash. In brush drawing, however, a graduated series of "washes," arranged from dark to light, is frequently prepared before work is even begun.

WATERCOLOR. Pigments mixed with water-soluble gum, usually applied in broad *washes* on white paper, unstained areas serving as *highlights* ("reserved lights"). Sometimes opaque watercolor ("body color") is added for color accents and highlights in areas already painted, but the essence of watercolor technique is transparency [*580, 791*]. A painting made primarily with opaque watercolor is called a "gouache" (gwahsh).

WESTWORK (fr. G. *Westwerk*; vest-verk). The broad, multistoried and turreted church front developed by Carolingian and Ottonian architects, including, variously, a western *transept*, *crossing* tower, *apse*, and stair turrets to upper galleries and *chapels* [*321–323, 329, 330*].

WOODCUT. A print made from a design raised in relief on a wooden block. All parts of the design which are not to be printed are cut away with knives and gouges; therefore it is a negative or subtractive process which does not directly register the lines made by the hand of the artist as in *engraving* and *etching* [fig. 20]. Sometimes, the designer and the cutter are different people; this was regularly the case in the preparation of Japanese woodcuts [*834*] which required still another man, a highly skilled printer, who inked and printed the separate color blocks used in making each print. Although the lines in woodcuts may imitate the elegant swelling and tapering of engraved lines [fig. 21a, *581*, *586*], they are usually thicker and more uniform [*465*]. The ink lies flat on the surface of the paper or may be slightly sunk into it by the pressure of the printing press, but the ink is never raised from the surface as in an engraving. In the relief process known as "wood-engraving," the method preferred for newspaper and book illustration during the nineteenth century, lines are cut with an engraver's *burin* into the end-grain of a very hard block of wood. The wood-engraver usually works positively, each cut printing as light on dark rather than dark on light as in woodcuts. Gauguin, although he worked on soft wood, used the positive cutting technique of the wood-engraver [*761*]. *See* BLOCK BOOK.

WORKSHOP. The apprentices and assistants who help an artist with his work, as well as the building or room in which they work, called "atelier" (at-lyay′) in France and "bottega" (bot-tay′ga) in Italy. In a large work-shop such as that of Raphael, Rubens, or Bernini, many people often worked on a single piece. The master might make a full-scale *cartoon* or a small-scale study, called a "modello" [*628*], from which his assistants would work in sketching out the final version which the master would then finish. A specialist in flower painting or animal painting might also be called in as needed. Many *hands* are often distinguishable in a large-scale work from a big work-shop. Sometimes one or more assistants might do all the work on a large picture, while only under the general supervision of the master; when this is the case, the piece is known as a "workshop production" or a "shop work." The value of a work usually depends on the degree of direct participation by the master, but this is often problematical and a matter of dispute among *connoisseurs*.

ZIGGURAT (zig′uh-rat; fr. Assyrian-Babylonian *ziqquratu*, mountain top). In Sumerian and Assyrian architecture, the high temple platform, built of mud brick, in the form of a truncated stepped pyramid with ramplike stairways leading to the sanctuary at the top [*68–71, 81*].

CHAPTER TWO

GODS, HEROES, AND MONSTERS

ABU, Sumerian god of vegetation. A statue of Abu, formerly in his temple (c. 2700–2500 B.C.) at Tell Asmar, has survived together with a group of statues of his priests and worshipers [*73*].

ACHILLES (uh-kil′eez), son of *Thetis* and *Peleus*, was the bravest and strongest of the Greek warriors sent against Troy.

ACIS (ay′sis), the lover of the beautiful sea-nymph *Galatea*. He was crushed under a rock thrown by the jealous giant *Polyphemus*, but his blood was transformed by Galatea into a river. One of the simulated easel pictures in Annibale Carracci's decoration of the gallery of the Farnese Palace in Rome [*603*] shows Polyphemus about to hurl the rock after the fleeing Acis.

AENEAS (eh-nee′us), Trojan hero who was forewarned by *Laocoön* of the fall of Troy and escaped to Italy where he founded the Roman nation. He is the ancestor of *Romulus* and *Remus* and ancestor of members of the Julian family, among them Caesar and the Emperor Augustus. The dolphin and Cupid at the base of the Primaporta statue of Augustus [Vatican, *224*] allude to the Emperor's supposed descent from Aeneas, who was the son of *Venus*.

AHRIMAN. In the dualistic Zoroastrian religion of the ancient Persians, the principle of evil and darkness. Ahriman is the opponent of *Ahuramazda* and the leader of evil spirits who are determined to destroy all that is good.

AHURAMAZDA. The Zoroastrian creator god and leader of the good spirits against the evil *Ahriman*. Ahuramazda is himself the principle of light, purity, truth and goodness.

ALCYONEUS (al-sai′oh-nus), one of the *Giants* who attacked the Greek gods. On the Altar of *Zeus* from Pergamum [Berlin, *180*], Alcyoneus is shown naked and winged; he struggles to free himself from *Athena* who pulls him by the hair as his mother *Gaea*, the earth goddess, watches in despair from below.

AMAZONS, a nation of fierce warrior women who were supposed by the Greeks to live in Asia Minor. Their battles with the Greeks, which they always lost, were a popular subject with Greek artists, who sometimes used the theme as a means of alluding to contemporary military victories [*169*].

AMUN (also Amen, Ammum, Ammon, Amon), an Egyptian wind god who was originally the local ram-headed deity of the city of Thebes, but was later united with the sun-god as Amun-Ra, the ruler of all the gods. A great temple [*60, 61*] begun c. 1390 B.C. by Amenhotep III at Luxor, across the Nile from Thebes, was dedicated to Amun, his wife *Mut*, and their son *Khonsu*. The oracle of Amun at Siwa in the Libyan desert was visited by Alexander the Great who was hailed as the son of Amun. Alexander appears with the horns of Amun on Hellenistic coins [*187*]; by associating himself with Amun, as the Pharaohs had done before him, he asserted his divine kingship. The Greeks and the Romans identified Amun with their supreme gods, *Zeus* and *Jupiter*, calling him Zeus-Ammon and Jupiter-Ammon.

ANTAEUS (an-tee'us). In Greek mythology, a Libyan giant, son of *Poseidon* and *Gaea* (Earth), who wrestled with *Herakles* (Hercules). Herakles, who discovered that Antaeus received his strength from contact with his mother, the Earth, lifted him off the ground and crushed him to death. The struggle, represented on Greek vases and coins, was revived as a subject, during the Renaissance, by Antonio del Pollaiuolo, who emphasized the violent action and tense musculature of the two wrestlers in a large (lost) painting for Lorenzo de' Medici, a little panel (Uffizi), and a small bronze [National Museum, Florence, *511*].

ANU (ah'noo), the Sumerian god of the sky. The "White Temple" atop the ziggurat at the Sumerian city of Uruk (c. 3500–3000 B.C.) [*68–70*] was probably dedicated to Anu.

APHRODITE (af-roh-dy'tee), the irresistible Greek goddess of Love, Beauty and fertility. The Romans identified her with *Venus*. According to one legend she sprang from the sea (*aphros* = sea foam), as in Botticelli's "Birth of Venus" [Uffizi, colorplate 36], a painting suggested by the great literary reputation of the lost Aphrodite Anadyomene (= rising from the sea) by Apelles, court painter of Alexander the Great. The pose of Botticelli's goddess is ultimately derived from such classical statues as Praxiteles' "Aphrodite of Cnidos" [Roman copy in the Vatican, *172*], renowned in antiquity for its perfection and for its nudity since the goddess had previously been represented as clothed. Cythera, near which Aphrodite was said to have risen from the sea, as well as Cnidos, was a center of her worship, and it is to this island that Watteau's lovers, in the painting in the Louvre [colorplate 55], make their pilgrimage.

APOLLO, the Greek and Roman god of the sun, music, poetry, healing, plagues, and prophecy, was the son of *Zeus* and Leto and the twin brother of *Artemis*. He is often called the "Delian Apollo" after his birthplace, the island of Delos. Other common epithets reveal his various rôles: as "Phoebus

(Radiant) Apollo" he is the god of the sun and is shown driving the sun-chariot across the heavens [604]; as "Apollo Musagetes" he is the leader of the *Muses*; and as the "Pythian Apollo" he is the Python Slayer and god of prophecy, since his famous oracle, called Pythia, was at Pytho (the old name for Delphi) where he killed the monstrous serpent Python. Apollo is represented as the most handsome of masterful young men; he has long golden locks and his beautiful body is usually only partially draped [156, 174, 195]. As the ideal image of the youthful god, the type was adopted for early representations of both Christ [264] and Buddha [837]. Apollo's special attributes are: the serpent Python [174, 242]; the wreath of laurel leaves [186] or the laurel tree [242] in honor of the chaste nymph Daphne who was turned into a laurel so that she might escape Apollo's embrace; the bow and arrows with which he sent plagues and slew Python, the *Giants* [132] and the *Niobids*; the lyre which he played as god of music and poetry [550]; and the tripod [242] in which his oracle sat at Delphi.

ARIADNE (ar-ee-ad'nee), the daughter of King Minos of Crete, who fell in love with the Athenian hero Theseus. She helped him escape from the Labyrinth of the *Minotaur* by giving him a ball of thread with which to find his way out again after killing the monster. They fled together from Crete, but Theseus abandoned Ariadne on the island of Naxos where she was discovered by *Dionysus* (Bacchus) who married her and gave her a crown which he set among the stars, as a constellation, upon her death. Ariadne frequently appears as the companion of Dionysus in representations of his drunken revels [colorplate 37]. In the frieze of the Dionysian rites in the Villa of the Mysteries at Pompeii [colorplate 10], the wine god blissfully lies in her lap as she enfolds him in her arms.

ARTEMIS (ahr'tuh-mis), daughter of *Zeus* and Leto, was the twin of *Apollo*. Artemis, like the Roman *Diana*, was goddess of the Moon and the proud virgin goddess of the Hunt. Tall, slender, and athletic, her attributes are the crescent moon and the bow and quiver. She is sometimes shown with her brother Apollo, who was also an archer, as they shoot their deadly arrows in depictions of the "Battle of the Gods and the *Giants*" [132] or the "Death of the *Niobids*." In many respects, Artemis, the moon goddess, is the female counterpart of her twin brother, the sun god: both were unwed, both healed the sick, but both also punished the wicked and sent plagues with their arrows.

ATEN (ah'ten), the sun god imposed upon Egypt as the one and only god by the monotheist Amenhotep IV [63], who changed his name to Akhenaten ("Aten-is-satisfied"). Aten was represented as a golden disc extending beneficent rays, each one terminating in a human hand. Some of the hands may offer an "ankh," the loop-topped cross which is the Egyptian symbol for "life."

ATHENA (uh-thee'nuh), Greek goddess of Wisdom and all the arts of civilization, including righteous warfare. Athena, who was the favorite child of *Zeus*, sprang full-grown and fully armed from his head: her miraculous birth was the main subject of the east pediment of the Parthenon [145], her chief temple on the Acropolis, the citadel of Athens. When Athena won possession of Attica in a contest with *Poseidon*, Athens, the principal city of the territory, was named after her. When coins were minted for the city, they bore her emblem, the owl. The Parthenon was dedicated to her as "Athena Parthenos" (Maiden) and contained the colossal gold and ivory statue, of the same name, by Phidias, but she was also worshiped as "Athena Nike" (Victory) in the Ionic temple overlooking the entrance to the Acropolis [*145, 147*], and as "Athena Polias" (of the city) in the eastern chamber of the Erechtheum [*145, 150*]. Phidias' great bronze statue of "Athena Promachus" (Champion) dominated the view as one passed up through the Propylaea, the monumental gateway to the Acropolis [145]. Every four years, as part of the Greater Panathenaea, Athena's chief festival, a procession, represented on the Parthenon frieze [*144, 163, 227*], wound up through the Propylaea [*146*] to wrap a richly embroidered robe (peplos) around the Athena Polias in the Erechtheum. Athena is represented as a fully draped mature and majestic woman wearing a helmet and holding a spear and shield; over her breast she wears the terrifying aegis (ee'jis), a short cloak or breastplate bearing the head of a *Gorgon* [*119, 134, 180, 550*]. *See* MINERVA.

AURORA, the Roman goddess of Dawn, identified with the Greek *Eos*. She is often shown riding across the sky in a chariot while scattering roses in allusion to her epithet "rosy-fingered Dawn" [*605*]. When Aurora is represented as the herald of *Apollo*, she flies ahead of his sun-chariot [*604*].

BACCHANTE (ba-kant'ee), one of the female followers of the Roman wine god Bacchus, noted for their gaiety, mad songs, and frenzied dancing [colorplate 41, *671*]. Their Greek counterparts, the ecstatic female companions of *Dionysus*, were called Maenads (mee'nadz).

BACCHUS (bak'us), the Latin name for the Greek wine god *Dionysus*, who was also sometimes called "Bakchos" by the Greeks.

BODHISATTVA. In Mahayana Buddhism, one of the divine beings who have renounced the ultimate goal of Nirvana to help save others and relieve the sufferings of mankind [*842*].

CENTAURS (sen'torz), a race of wild creatures, half man and half horse, living in Thessaly in northern Greece. Their animal natures dominate their actions, which are marked by sudden violence. Invited to the wedding festivities of Hippodamia and Pirithous, king of the *Lapiths*, the centaurs, as usual, drank too much and attacked the bride and her guests. The ensuing battle, which resulted in the rout of the centaurs, was frequently represented in Greek art [*121, 157*], sometimes as a moral lesson demonstrating the conquest of reason over passion or the victory of the Greeks over the Persians.

CEPHALUS (sef'uh-lus), son of *Hermes* and Herse, was married to Procris, daughter of *Erechtheus*, but Eos (Aurora), the goddess of Dawn, abducted him. Cephalus, proclaiming his love for Procris, at first rejected her advances [*653*], but yielded after putting his wife's fidelity to a test devised by Eos. Disguised as a handsome stranger, he returned to Procris and, to his grief, successfully seduced her. Later, Cephalus killed the jealous Procris with a spear, mistaking her for an animal as she spied upon him from a thicket.

CERBERUS (ser'ber-us) was the three-headed watchdog who guarded the entrance to *Hades* [*193*].

COATLICUE (koh-at-lee'kway), the Aztec earth goddess, was also the goddess of death and mother of the war god Huitzilopochtli. The terrible aspect of the goddess is seen in her monumental stone statue in Mexico City [*846*]: she wears the skirt woven of serpents after which she is named (Coatlicue = "serpent-skirt"); a necklace of human hands and hearts with a pendant skull adorns her broad chest; and her head is composed of two rattlesnakes rising, in profile, from her shoulders.

CUPID or AMOR, son of *Venus*, was the Roman counterpart of the Greek god of Love, Eros, son of *Aphrodite*. He is represented as a handsome winged youth or as a mischievous toddler [*224*]: his attributes are the quiver and bow which he uses in shooting his darts of love [*587*]. When one or more winged *putti* appear with the attributes of Cupid, they are called "cupids" or "amoretti" [*551*, colorplate 50].

CYBELE (sib'uh-lee), the great mother goddess of Phrygia in Asia Minor. She was called "Mother of the Gods" and, when the performance of her fertility rites spread to Greece, she was identified with Rhea, daughter of *Gaea*, and mother of the Olympian gods. She wears a crown in the form of a turreted wall, symbolizing her rôle as protectress in time of war, and she is often shown standing in a chariot drawn by lions [*132*], symbolizing her position as goddess of wild nature.

CYCLOPES (sai'klohp-eez), a race of one-eyed giants who lived in Sicily. Some were shepherds like *Polyphemus*, the most famous Cyclops; others helped Hephaestus (Vulcan), the divine blacksmith, forge the thunderbolts of *Zeus* beneath fiery Mount Aetna. In tribute to the great strength of the Cyclopes, walls of enormous stones, such as those at Mycenae [*111*], are sometimes called "Cyclopean".

DEMETER (duh-mee'ter), Greek goddess of grain, agriculture, and fertility. She is represented as a fully clothed, mature, and dignified woman [*171*]. Her attributes are ears or sheaves of grain.

DIANA, the ancient Italian moon goddess, was later identified with the Greek *Artemis*.

DIONYSUS (dy-uh-ny'sus), the Greek wine god, called *Bacchus* by the Romans, was the son of *Zeus* and Semele. Before Dionysus was born, however, Semele was killed by the thunderbolts of Zeus when she insisted that her divine lover appear to her in his full majesty as king of the gods. Zeus snatched the unborn child from her womb and kept it sewed up in his thigh until it was ready to be born. Then *Hermes* carried the infant to the nymphs of Nysa [*173*] who raised him. *Silenus* was his tutor and helped him discover the art of making wine, which Dionysus, accompanied by his wife *Ariadne*, Silenus, and his band of Maenads (*Bacchantes*) and *satyrs* (fauns), introduced to the peoples of the world. He also introduced many of the other early arts of civilization such as bee-keeping [colorplate 37] and was regarded as the patron of song and drama. Each year at Athens he was honored in the festival of the Great Dionysia for which Aeschylus, Sophocles, Euripedes, and Aristophanes wrote their great plays. Dionysus and his companions appear on thousands of Greek vases which were used for storing, drinking, and mixing wine. On the older vases he is represented as a majestic bearded old man [*120*]; later, however, he is portrayed as a handsome, semi-nude, and sometimes rather girlish youth [*161*, colorplates 10, 37]. His special attributes are ivy and the grapevine, which he wears as a wreath, the thyrsus (a staff topped by a bunch of ivy leaves) [colorplate 10], and the special form of wine cup called a "kantharos," which has two large handles looping high above the lip of the bowl [*185*] and usually a tall stem and broad circular base.

EOS (ee'os), Greek goddess of Dawn, called *Aurora* by the Romans. After driving her chariot across the sky each morning [*605*], Eos spent much of her time pursuing and carrying off handsome young men, among them *Cephalus* [*653*] and Tithonus, the brother of King Priam of Troy. By Tithonus she became the mother of *Memnon* whose death during the Trojan War was the greatest grief of her life [*122*].

ERECHTHEUS (eh-rek'thoos *or* eh-rek'thee-us), legendary king of Athens, was the son of *Gaea* and the fire god Hephaestus, but he was raised by *Athena*. The Erechtheum [*145, 150*], in which Erechtheus, Athena, *Poseidon*, and Hephaestus were worshiped, marks the spot on the Acropolis where Erechtheus judged the contest of Athena and Poseidon for possession of Athens. Athena gave the Athenians the olive tree which was judged more valuable than Poseidon's gifts of the horse and a spring of salt water. In honor of the new protectress of the city, Erechtheus instituted the Panathenaic festival which was celebrated with athletic and musical contests and the great procession represented on the frieze of the Parthenon [*144, 163, 227*].

EUROPA (yoo-roh'puh), a Phoenician princess, was playing by the seashore with her friends one day when *Zeus* approached her in the form of a handsome white bull. Charmed by the gentle bull, Europa sat on his back, as he kneeled before her, and was carried off to Crete where she bore Zeus three sons, among them King Minos.

FAME. In classical and Renaissance art, fame is usually personified as a winged female figure holding or blowing a long trumpet [*625, 628, 662*].

FAUN. In Roman mythology, one of the lustful creatures of the forest—half goat and half man—who join in the revels of *Bacchus* and spend much of their time drinking wine and annoying the *Bacchantes* [*176*, colorplate 37]. Fauns are Roman counterparts of the Greek *satyrs*.

FORTUNA, the Roman goddess of Chance and Happiness, whose attributes are the horn of plenty (symbolizing the bounty she can bestow), a ball (indicating her instability), and a rudder with which she steers men's fates. Her oracle could be consulted at Praeneste (Palestrina), southeast of Rome, where a vast sanctuary honoring her as "Fortuna Primigenia" (the first-born child of *Jupiter*) was built in the early first century B.C. [*202–204*].

GAEA (jee'uh), the Greek earth goddess who sprang directly from Chaos.

She was both the mother and spouse of the sky god Uranus by whom she conceived the *Giants* and *Cyclopes*. The Roman equivalent of Gaea was *Tellus*.

GALATEA (gal'uh-tee'uh), the beautiful sea nymph [*551*] who loved *Acis*, but was relentlessly pursued by the enamored Cyclops *Polyphemus*. Galatea was one of the fifty daughters of the sea god Nereus, the Old Man of the Sea, who were called Nereïds (nee'ree-idz).

GANYMEDE (gan'ih-meed). The youthful cup bearer of the gods, renowned for his beauty. According to Ovid, *Zeus*, disguised as an eagle, swooped down on Ganymede one day and carried him off to Olympus and immortality [*603*]. Renaissance Neo-Platonists interpreted the myth as an allegory of the ascent of the soul to heaven.

GENIUS. In classical and Renaissance art, a spirit represented in human form, often semi-nude and winged, who acts as a protector of a person, a people, or a place. Genii are often merely decorative [*229, 509*], but they may also appear as personifications of important abstract concepts, as the Genius of Liberty [*732*] or the Genius of the Roman People [*232*].

GIANTS, the great and powerful sons of *Gaea* who piled Mount Pelion on top of Mount Ossa to scale Olympus and attack the gods. After a great battle (the Gigantomachy), during which *Herakles* came to the aid of the gods, the Giants were overcome and buried beneath volcanoes throughout Greece and Italy [*132, 180*]. *See* ALCYONEUS.

GORGONS. In Greek mythology, female monsters whose hideous gaze turned men to stone. They are usually represented with frightfully large heads and writhing snakes for hair [*117, 130, 131*]. The most famous Gorgon was *Medusa*.

HADES (hay'deez). In Greek mythology, the lord of the Underworld whose name was synonymous with his realm, the abode of the spirits of the dead. The spirits were escorted by *Hermes* to the banks of the River Styx where they had to pay the boatman Charon to ferry them across to the entrance of the Underworld. The entrance was guarded by the monster *Cerberus* who let everyone in but no one out. Hades ruled the Underworld with his wife Persephone, daughter of *Zeus* and *Demeter*, the goddess of Agriculture. Hades surprised Persephone one day while she was picking flowers and carried her off to the Underworld. She was permitted to return to the upper world each spring, but had to return to Hades during the winter. This myth, like that of the annual death and return of the Babylonian god *Tammuz*, serves to explain the death and regeneration of plant life each year.

HERA (hee'ruh), sister and wife of *Zeus* and queen of the Greek gods, was the protectress of women. Her Roman counterpart was *Juno*. Hera was worshiped from early times on the island of Samos, which the Samians claimed as her birthplace. The famous Archaic statue in the Louvre called the "Hera of Samos" [*128*] was found in her sanctuary there.

HERAKLES (herr'uh-kleez), the most famous of the Greek heroes, was renowned for his courage and his superhuman strength. He was the son of Alcmene by *Zeus*, who visited her in the form of her husband, Amphitryon of Thebes. Although "Herakles" means "Hera's glory," the hero was hated by the jealous *Hera* who sent a fit of madness upon him during which he killed his children. Seeking expiation, Herakles consulted the Delphic oracle and was sent to serve King Eurystheus of Tiryns who commanded him to perform the famous Twelve Labors. Some of his more famous labors were strangling the Nemean lion [*119*, colorplate 5], cleaning the stables of King Augeas which had been befouled by three thousand cattle for thirty years, bringing back the golden apples of the Hesperides (the daughters of Atlas), and capturing *Cerberus*, the watchdog of *Hades*. Herakles is represented as powerful, muscular, and even brutish. He is frequently bearded; he carries a great club, and wears or carries a lion's skin [*249, 511*]. Sometimes he wears the lion's head as a helmet [*135*].

HERCULES (her'kyoo-leez), the Roman name for *Herakles*.

HERMES (her'meez), the herald of the Greek gods, who was noted for his persuasiveness and shrewd trickery. Since he was the god of Commerce, he was identified by the Romans with their *Mercury*. His attributes are the caduceus (ka-doo'see-us; a herald's rod entwined by serpents), winged sandals, and a winged cap. Although originally represented as bearded and muscular, by the fourth century B.C., Hermes is young, slender, and beardless [*173*].

HORUS, Egyptian god of Light and Day who was incarnate in each Pharaoh. He is represented as a falcon [*41, 51*] or falcon-headed man.

IO (ai'oh), daughter of the river god Inachus, was ravished by *Zeus* (Jupiter) who visited her in a dark cloud. To conceal Io's identity from his jealous wife *Hera*, Zeus transformed her into a heifer, which Hera later had relentlessly pursued from country to country by a gadfly. Even when Io is represented in human form, there is often the suggestion of small horns projecting from her temples [*563*].

IPHIGENIA (if'ih-juh-nai'uh), the daughter of the Mycenaean king Agamemnon who prepared to sacrifice her to *Artemis* so that the goddess would release the Greek fleet which was becalmed off Aulis while on its way to war against Troy [*291*]. At the last minute, however, Artemis substituted a hind for Iphigenia and transported her to Tauris (the Crimea) to be her priestess.

ISHTAR, the Babylonian mother goddess, whose murder and resurrection of her lover *Tammuz* is a symbol of death and regeneration. Each year, when Ishtar descends into the Underworld to retrieve Tammuz, the fertility of the earth is suspended, but, with the return of the goddess and her lover, it is restored. In the city wall of Babylon, near the palace of Nebuchadnezzar (604–562 B.C.), a great gate [*86*], dedicated to Ishtar, opened onto the main processional street which was lined with life-size reliefs in glazed brick of her sacred beast—the lion.

JUNO, the wife of *Jupiter* and queen of the Roman gods, was identified with the Greek *Hera*.

JUPITER, the Italian sky god, who became wholly identified with the Greek *Zeus* as king of the gods.

KHONSU, Egyptian moon god, son of *Amun* and *Mut*. All three were known as the Theban Triad and were worshiped together in the great temple at Luxor [*60, 61*], across the Nile from Thebes. At Karnak, each member of the triad had a separate temple [fig. 39].

LAESTRIGONIANS, the race of man-eating giants who smashed the fleet of *Odysseus* (Ulysses) by hurling huge rocks [colorplate 9]. Only Odysseus' own ship, which was anchored outside the narrow entrance to their harbor, managed to escape.

LAOCOÖN (lay-ok'oh-on), the priest of *Apollo* who warned the Trojans not to take the Wooden Horse, in which the Greeks lay concealed, into their city. To discredit Laocoön and permit the entry of the Greeks and the consequent destruction of Troy, *Athena* had the priest and his two sons crushed to death by two monstrous serpents from the sea [*182*].

LAPITHS (lap'iths). In Greek mythology, a people of Thessaly in northern Greece who defeated the *Centaurs* in the battle which was represented on the west pediment of the Temple of Zeus at Olympia [*157*], on the metopes of the Parthenon, and on the Mausoleum at Harlicarnassus [*168*].

MAENAD. *See* BACCHANTE.

MARS, the Roman war god, was originally a god of agricultural fertility after whom the month of March was named. He was highly revered by the Romans as the father of *Romulus*, the founder of Rome. The Greek counterpart of Mars was Ares.

MEDUSA (meh-doo'suh), one of the snake-haired *Gorgons* who turned to stone all those who looked at them. Medusa was beheaded by *Perseus*.

MEMNON, king of Ethiopia, the son of *Eos* (Aurora) and Tithonus, came to the aid of his uncle, King Priam of Troy, during the Trojan War, but was finally slain by *Achilles*. His mother, the goddess of Dawn, was so grief-stricken that she threatened to leave the world in darkness [*122*]. *Zeus* granted Memnon immortality, but each morning Eos still weeps tears of dew.

MERCURY, the Roman god of Commerce, became identified with the Greek *Hermes*, the messenger of the Olympian gods.

MINERVA, goddess of Wisdom and patroness of arts and crafts, was, with *Jupiter* and *Juno*, one of the three deities most highly honored by the Romans. She absorbed the mythology and attributes of her Greek counterpart *Athena*.

MINOTAUR (min'uh-tor; fr. Gk. *Minotauros*, Minos' bull). The monster with the body of a man and the head of a bull which was kept by King Minos of Crete in the Labyrinth built by his architect Daedalus. The beast was born to Pasiphaë, the wife of Minos, as a result of her unnatural union with a bull which *Poseidon* had given to Minos with the understanding that it would be sacrificed to him. Instead, Minos kept the bull and the Minotaur was his punishment. Each year, Athens paid tribute to Minos by sending seven youths and seven maidens which the Minotaur devoured. The Minotaur was finally killed by the Athenian hero Theseus who was aided by Minos' daughter *Ariadne*.

MUSES (myoo'zez), the Greek goddesses of the arts and sciences who inspired poets and authors. *Apollo*, as god of music and poetry, was their leader and they assembled with him near the inspiring waters of the Castalian Spring on Mount Parnassus where they are shown in one of Raphael's frescoes in the "Stanza della Segnatura" in the Vatican. Nine Muses are generally recognized: (1) Calliope, Muse of Epic Poetry, usually shown holding a tablet and stylus. (2) Clio, Muse of History, holds a scroll or book. (3) Erato, Muse of Love Poetry, sometimes holds a lyre. (4) Euterpe, Muse of Music, holds a flute. (5) Melpomene, Muse of Tragedy, wears an ivy wreath and carries a tragic mask and a sword or the club of *Herakles*. (6) Polyhymnia, Muse of Sacred Song, is veiled and contemplative. (7) Terpsichore, Muse of Dancing, plays the lyre. (8) Thalia, Muse of Comedy, wears an ivy wreath and holds a comic mask and a shepherd's staff. (9) Urania, Muse of Astronomy, holds a rod and a globe. Our word "museum" ("place of the Muses") derives from the association of the Muses with the arts and sciences.

MUT, the vulture-headed mother (mut) of the Egyptian gods, wife of *Amun* and queen of the heavens. The great temple at Luxor [*60, 61*], near Thebes, was dedicated to Amun, Mut, and their son *Khonsu*, who were known as the "Theban Triad."

NEPTUNE, Roman god of the Sea, was identified with the Greek *Poseidon* and was represented with the same attributes.

NIKE (nee'kay *or* nai'kee), the Greek goddess of Victory, called "Victoria" by the Romans. She is represented as a draped, winged woman and is often shown flying or with wind-blown drapery [*181*]. Her attributes are the palm branch or a laurel wreath which she may hold over the head of the victor [*180, 232, 662*]. Sometimes a number of victories, or nikai, may be represented in a single composition as on the balustrade of the Temple of Athena Nike on the Acropolis [*164*].

NIOBE (nai'oh-bee), a queen of Thebes, whose overbearing pride in her seven sons and seven daughters led her to refuse to worship Leto (Latona), the mother of only two. Leto punished her by sending her own two children, the archers *Apollo* and *Artemis*, to kill all fourteen of Niobe's children (the *Niobids*) with their arrows [*160*]. Niobe, frozen with grief, was turned into a stone by *Zeus*, but the stone was always wet with her tears.

NIOBIDS (nai'oh-bidz), the children of *Niobe*, who were killed by *Apollo* and *Artemis* to punish the pride of their mother.

NYMPH. In Greek and Roman mythology, one of the countless minor female nature deities. Each tree, grove, grotto, stream, rock and region could have its own attendant nymph. As their name ("young woman") implies, nymphs are represented as young and beautiful; they are usually lightly clad and carry attributes, such as flowers or water jars, which are appropriate to their province [*599, 600*]. They are usually kind to strangers but some have a lascivious nature and abduct handsome young men. Nymphs, in turn, are frequently pursued by satyrs and courted by men and gods alike. *Achilles*, for example, was the son of *Peleus*, a mortal, and the sea nymph *Thetis*.

ODYSSEUS (oh-dis'us, called "Ulysses" by the Romans), the wily hero of Homer's "Odyssey." After fighting for ten years in the Trojan War, it took

Odysseus another ten years of wandering and hardship before he was able to return to his kingdom of Ithaca and his faithful wife Penelope. Most of his troubles on his return from Troy stemmed from his blinding of *Polyphemus*, the *Cyclops*, who sought vengeance through his father *Poseidon*. This and other adventures, such as the destruction of his fleet by the *Laestrigonians*, were frequently represented by Greek and Roman painters [*117*, colorplate 9].

ORPHEUS (or'fee-us), son of *Apollo* and the *Muse* Calliope, who sang and played his lyre so beautifully that he charmed the birds and beasts and even the trees and stones followed after him. When Orpheus descended into *Hades* to seek his wife Eurydice (yoo-rid'uh-see), the gods and demons were so moved by his plaintive song that they permitted him to return with his wife under the condition that he not look back at her on the way to the upper world. As they were about to leave the Underworld, Orpheus turned to see whether Eurydice was still following him and thus lost her forever.

PAN, the mischievous Greek god of the Arcadian woods and fields, was the protector of flocks and herds and had the power to "panic" all those who threatened his charges. Pan, whom the Romans associated with the wood god Faunus, is represented as a *satyr* (faun) and like the satyrs is often shown in the company of *Dionysus* (Bacchus). He is distinguished from them by his shepherd's crook and the Panpipe, or "syrinx," which he fashioned from reeds of unequal length [*249*] when the nymph Syrinx, whom he was pursuing, was turned into a bed of reeds to escape his embrace.

PARIS, son of Queen Hecuba and King Priam of Troy, was abandoned by his parents because of a prophecy that he would be the ruin of Troy. However, he was rescued by shepherds and reared on Mount Ida where he was chosen by *Zeus* to decide the dispute among *Aphrodite, Hera*, and *Athena* [*587*] as to which one of them deserved the golden apple, inscribed "For the Fairest," which the goddess of Discord had thrown among them at the wedding of *Peleus* and *Thetis*. Hera promised Paris that he would be ruler of all Asia if he decided in her favor; Athena promised him wisdom and glory in battle; and Aphrodite promised him the most beautiful woman in the world. Paris gave the apple to Aphrodite and later carried off Helen, the wife of King Menelaus of Sparta, as his reward. This act, which was the cause of the Trojan War, ultimately resulted in his own death and the destruction of Troy.

PELEUS (pee'lee-us), king of the Myrmidons of Thessaly and father of *Achilles* by the sea-nymph *Thetis*, whom he took by force [*167*]. At the wedding festivities for Peleus and Thetis, the dispute which ultimately led to the Judgment of *Paris* and the Trojan War was started when Eris, the goddess of Discord, who was furious at not having been invited, cunningly threw a golden apple, inscribed with the words "For the Fairest" among the guests.

PERSEUS (per'see-us) was the son of Danaë, daughter of King Acrisius of Argos, whom *Zeus* visited in a shower of gold. Acrisius, to prevent the fulfilment of a prophecy that he would be killed by his grandson, put Danaë and her baby into a chest and had it thrown into the sea. The chest drifted to the island of Seriphus where they were rescued by a fisherman. Polydectes, the ruler of Seriphus, fell in love with Danaë who resisted his advances. Wishing to rid himself of Perseus, who had grown up and now stood in his way, Polydectes commanded Perseus to bring back the head of the Gorgon *Medusa*, whose gaze turned men to stone. Managing to decapitate Medusa while watching her reflection in his shield, Perseus returned with the head to Polydectes and turned him to stone. Arriving at Argos with his mother and his bride Andromeda, whom he had rescued from a monster while on his way back to Seriphus, Perseus found that his grandfather Acrisius had fled out of fear of the prophecy that the son of Danaë would kill him. Perseus set out to persuade Acrisius to return, but, while participating in funeral games at Larissa, in Thessaly, he threw a discus which accidentally struck and killed a man in the crowd. The man was Acrisius.

POLYPHEMUS (pol'ih-fee'mus), the ugly man-eating *Cyclops* who fell in love with the sea nymph *Galatea* and slew her lover *Acis* [*603*]. Polyphemus' single eye was gouged out by *Odysseus* and his men after the giant trapped them in his cave and began eating them two at a time [*117*].

PORTUNUS, the Roman god of Harbors. The Ionic temple by the Tiber in Rome [*200*], formerly called "Fortuna Virilis," may have been dedicated to Portunus.

POSEIDON (poh-sai'dun), the Greek god of water and the sea, took possession of his realm when he and his brothers, *Zeus* and *Hades*, divided the universe among themselves after they had defeated their father Cronus (Saturn). Hades received the Underworld and Zeus, the sky; the land was common to all. Poseidon took up residence at the bottom of the sea, but repeatedly tried to extend his dominion to the land, as in his contest with *Athena* for possession of Attica. When Poseidon travels, his entourage is as numerous as that of *Dionysus* and usually far more stately [*628*]. He often rides in a splendid chariot drawn by horses or hippocamps (horses with fishtails) and is accompanied by splashing dolphins, curious creatures of the deep, and a multitude of sea gods [*6*], among them, perhaps, Nereus and his daughters (the Nereïds) or Oceanus and his daughters (the Oceanids) or Amphitrite, Poseidon's wife, and their son Triton, who uses a shell as a trumpet. Poseidon, like his brother Zeus, is represented as a powerful bearded figure [*158*], but he is distinguished from Zeus by his special attribute, the trident [*567*], the three-pronged spear with which he strikes forth horses and springs, shakes the earth, raises tempests, or calms the sea.

PUTTO (poo'toh; It., boy; *pl.* putti). The chubby little nude boys, usually winged, who frequently lend an air of levity to classical and Renaissance paintings and sculpture [*509, 514, 604, 605*]. When they carry bows and arrows, they are personifications of love and are called "cupids" or "amoretti" [*551*, colorplate 50].

RA (rah), the Egyptian sun god, was called "first king of Egypt" and the Pharaohs were thought to be his descendants. The obelisk and the solar disk were his emblems. The worship of Ra was originally centered at Heliopolis, but during the second millenium B.C. he became identified through a process of syncretism with *Amun*, the local god of Thebes, capital of the Egyptian Empire, and as Amun-Ra became the supreme god of all Egypt.

REMUS, twin brother of *Romulus*, the legendary founder of Rome. Soon after they were born, the twin brothers, who were sons of *Mars* and the vestal virgin Rhea Silvia, were set adrift on the Tiber by Amulius, who had seized the throne of Alba Longa from his brother Numitor, Silvia's father. The babies were washed ashore and found by a she-wolf who suckled them in her den [*196*]. Raised by a shepherd, the twins grew up and killed Amulius, restoring Numitor to the throne. They then set out to found a new city, but fell to quarreling over where it should be built and after whom it should be named. Romulus settled the dispute by killing his brother and naming the town after himself.

ROMULUS, twin brother of *Remus*, and legendary founder of Rome. Romulus laid out the walls of Rome on the Palatine Hill and attracted men to the new town by setting aside an asylum for fugitives on the neighboring Capitoline Hill. After the men seized wives for themselves in the Rape of the Sabine Women [*569, 654*], a war broke out between the Romans and the *Sabines*, but when the wives threw themselves between the opposing armies it was decided to unite the Sabines and Romans under the joint rule of Romulus and Titus Tatius, the Sabine king. After the death of Tatius, Romulus alone ruled over both peoples and, at the end of a long reign, was carried to heaven by his father *Mars*. Thereafter he was worshiped as a god under the name of Quirinus.

SABINES (say'bines), an ancient people of the Sabine Hills, northeast of Rome. According to legend, *Romulus*, the founder of Rome, in order to provide wives for his men, invited the Sabines to a festival in the new settlement. During the festivities, the Romans seized the Sabine women and drove off their men [*569, 654*].

SATYR (say'ter). One of the rustic creatures with the body of a man and the shaggy legs of a goat who are boisterous and lustful companions of *Dionysus*. Satyrs, like their Roman counterparts, the *fauns*, are represented with pointed ears, two horns and a tail [colorplate 37, *671*].

SHAMASH (shah'mahsh), the Babylonian sun god and supreme judge. King Hammurabi, the "favorite shepherd" of Shamash, appears before the throne of his god at the top of the stele inscribed with his famous code of laws [Louvre, *79*].

SIBYL (sib'ill). In Greek and Roman mythology, the prophetess, inspired by *Apollo*, who lived in a cave at Cumae in southern Italy. In time, as many as twelve "sibyls" came to be recognized, among them the Persian, Erythraean, Delphic, and Libyan sibyls who share places of honor with the Cumaean Sibyl and the prophets of the Old Testament on Michelangelo's Sistine Ceiling because they were thought to have foretold the coming of Christ [*538*].

SILENI (sy'lee-ny), minor woodland deities in the entourage of *Dionysus* (Bacchus). Like *Silenus*, they are snub-nosed and thick-lipped and share his passion for wine. Sileni are distinguished from the goat-like *satyrs* by their horse's ears and tails; they are sometimes represented with horse's legs as well, but they are usually essentially human in form except for their ears and tails [*185*].

SILENUS (sy-lee´nus), the jolly old fat man who was the tutor and constant companion of the wine god *Dionysus* (Bacchus). Silenus is usually so befuddled with wine that he must be supported by *satyrs* or ride on an ass [colorplate 37]. Despite his drunkenness—or because of it—he was noted for his wisdom and prophetic powers. In the frieze of the Villa of the Mysteries near Pompeii [colorplate 10], Silenus and a satyr, who peers into the silver wine cup which the old man holds, may be practicing an ancient method of prophecy whereby the future is seen in a vessel filled with a liquid.

SIVA or SHIVA (shee´vuh), Hindu god of destruction and procreation, one of the gods of the Trimurti, or trinity, which also includes Brahma the Creator and Vishnu the Preserver. As Nataraja ("Lord of the Dance"), Siva personifies the cosmic process of creation and destruction and is represented with two or more pairs of arms as though in perpetual movement [*843*].

SPHINX, a creature with the body of a lion and the head of a man or a woman. A double row of sphinxes was placed before Egyptian temples to form a grand avenue leading to the entrance [fig. 39]. The head of the Great Sphinx at Giza may have been intended as a portrait of the Pharaoh Chefren [cf. *50* and *51*]. Sphinxes, frequently represented with the breasts of a woman, appear as decorative features in classical and Renaissance art [*225, 603*] and may sometimes allude to the Sphinx sent against Thebes by *Hera* and vanquished by Oedipus who solved the riddle it posed.

TAMMUZ (tam´mooz), the Sumerian fertility god of flocks, herds, crops and vegetation, whose annual death in the autumn and rebirth in the spring symbolized the cycle of nature. Tammuz, who was called "leading goat of the land" in honor of his generative powers, may be symbolically represented in the gold-covered stands for offering tables, carved in the form of a rearing goat resting his forefeet against a flowering tree, which have been excavated at Ur [colorplate 3]. *See* ISHTAR.

TELEPHUS (tel´uh-fus), the son of *Herakles* (Hercules) and Auge (aw´jee), a priestess of *Athena*, who, in her shame, left the baby to die on Mount Parthenius in Arcadia. Telephus, however, was suckled by a hind [*249*] and years later, according to one legend, was about to marry his mother when her identity was miraculously revealed at the last minute.

TELLUS, or Terra Mater (Mother Earth), was identified by the Romans with the Greek earth goddess *Gaea*. She was the goddess of marriage and the fertility of flocks and fields. On the Ara Pacis (Altar of Peace) of the Emperor Augustus [*230*], she sits among plants and animals and holds two babies in her fruit-filled lap; to either side of her are the personified elements of Air and Water. Tellus also appears on another important Augustan work: the Primaporta statue of Augustus himself [Vatican, *224*]; here Tellus appears at the bottom of the breastplate as a reclining figure holding a cornucopia and looming protectively over two babies. Considering the propagandistic function of these two works as emblems of the peace and prosperity of the

Augustan age, the babies may very well have been intended to represent the Roman twins, *Romulus* and *Remus*.

THETIS (thee'tis), one of the fifty daughters of the sea-god Nereus who were called Nereïds (nee'ree-idz). The gods allowed Thetis to be abducted by *Peleus* [*167*], a mortal, when it was learned that her son was to be mightier than his father. The son was *Achilles*, the great Greek hero of the Trojan War, the seeds of which were sown at Thetis' wedding when the Apple of Discord was thrown among the guests.

VENUS, an ancient Italian goddess of Spring and vegetation, was only a minor deity until the Romans identified her with the Greek *Aphrodite* as the goddess of Love and Beauty. As the mother of *Aeneas*, who was the ancestor of *Romulus*, the founder of Rome, she was revered as the ancestress of the Roman People. Julius Caesar, whose family claimed descent from Aeneas, dedicated a temple to her as "Venus Genetrix" (Ancestress) in his forum at Rome [*205*]. The little *Cupid* riding a dolphin at the base of the Primaporta statue of the Emperor Augustus [Vatican, *224*], who was adopted by Caesar, symbolizes the divine descent of the Julian family since Cupid was the son of Venus and the dolphin alludes to the birth of Venus from the sea [colorplate 36]. In the "Garden of Love" by Rubens [Prado, colorplate 50], where Venus appears as a fountain of fertility, the goddess herself rides a dolphin. In Watteau's "Pilgrimage to Cythera" [colorplate 55], her presence is also marked by a statue; it is entwined with roses, her sacred flower. The apple which Venus sometimes holds [*730*] is the prize awarded to her by *Paris* in recognition of her supreme beauty [*587*].

YAKSHIS (yahk'sheez), the opulently endowed female fertility spirits who were absorbed from the ancient Hindu religion into the Buddhist pantheon [*839*]. The male counterpart of a yakshi is called a "yaksha" (yahk'shuh).

ZEPHYR or ZEPHYRUS (zef'ih-rus), the Greek personification of the gentle West Wind, was the son of *Eos* (Aurora). He married Chloris (Flora), the goddess of flowers and Spring. In Botticelli's "Birth of Venus" [Uffizi, colorplate 36], the winged Zephyr wafts the newborn goddess as he glides through the air, embracing a wind goddess with one arm and scattering flowers with the other.

ZEUS (zoos), the supreme god of the ancient Greek religion, was identified by the Romans with *Jupiter*. He was the great father of the gods and men, who enforced the moral law and could crush all who defied him. Zeus was the son of the Titan Cronus (Saturn) and the Titaness Rhea who were the children of the sky god Uranus and the earth goddess *Gaea*. Cronus castrated his father Uranus with a sickle given to him by his mother Gaea, who was angry with Uranus for banishing their monstrous children, the *Cyclopes*. As Uranus lay dying, he prophesied that Cronus, in turn, would be overthrown by one of his own children. To prevent this, Cronus ate each of his children as they were born. This was the fate of Hestia (goddess of the Hearth), *Demeter, Hera, Hades,* and *Poseidon*, but Rhea hid her sixth child, Zeus, with Gaea and gave her husband a stone wrapped in swaddling clothes to eat in place of the baby. When Zeus was fully grown, he forced Cronus to disgorge his brothers and sisters who made war on their father and overthrew him. Zeus, Hades, and Poseidon then divided the universe among themselves. The sky became the special province of Zeus and he built his palace atop Mount Olympus, the highest mountain in Greece, but he was more powerful than all the other gods put together and became supreme ruler of the entire universe. He married his sister Hera, who, as queen, had considerable power, but could not prevent her husband's notorious infidelities [*563*]. Zeus is represented as a majestic, bearded figure [*158*], whose special attributes are his mighty thunderbolts and his messenger, the eagle. In antiquity, the most famous representation of Zeus was the colossal seated figure of ivory and gold made by Phidias for the great temple at Olympia where, every four years, athletes assembled from all parts of the Greek world to participate in the games held in honor of the one god they all worshiped as supreme.

PARALLEL *Greek* AND Roman GODS

Aphrodite	/	Venus	*Eros*	/	Cupid or Amor
Apollo	/	Apollo	*Gaea*	/	Tellus
Ares	/	Mars	*Hades*	/	Pluto
Artemis	/	Diana	*Hera*	/	Juno
Athena	/	Minerva	*Hermes*	/	Mercury
Demeter	/	Ceres	*Poseidon*	/	Neptune
Dionysus	/	Bacchus	*Tyche*	/	Fortuna
Eos	/	Aurora	*Zeus*	/	Jupiter

CHAPTER THREE

CHRISTIAN SUBJECTS

DEVOTIONAL SUBJECTS

THE TRINITY. Although God the Father, God the Son, and God the Holy Ghost are three persons of one and the same God, who may be represented by a single figure, each person of the Trinity has his own individuality, both theologically and in representations in art. God the Father, the Creator, was at first represented simply by a *hand* issuing from a cloud [colorplate 20], sometimes he appeared as a head or a bust [*358*], and, later, as a full-length figure of a rather old man with a long beard [*479, 539*]. Jesus Christ, in the words of the Nicene Creed, is "the only-begotten Son of God, born of the Father before all ages; God of God; Light of Light; true God of true God; begotten not made; consubstantial with the Father, by whom all things were made." In Early Christian art, he appears as the Good Shepherd [*252*; cf. Luke 15: 3–7; John 10: 1–18] and sometimes he is represented by the cross alone—the most common symbol of his sacrifice—even in narrative scenes [colorplate 13]. While the Son proceeds from the Father, the Holy Ghost proceeds from both the Father and the Son and is that person of the Trinity still immanent in the world, sent to inspire the Apostles and the Church during *Pentecost*. The *dove* has remained, since Early Christian times, the universal symbol of the Holy Ghost. The Trinity as a whole is now usually represented by abstract figures such as the *trefoil* or *triangle*, but, at times, three separate but identical figures have been used, as in depictions of the three angels received by Abraham [*288*; Genesis 18], who were interpreted as prefiguring the Trinity. The most common representations of the Trinity as a separate subject, however, are those showing God the Father as an older man sitting or standing with Christ, who holds the cross or is actually crucified, while the Dove of the Holy Ghost hovers between them [*492*].

THE PANTOCRATOR. The awesome image of Christ the Pantocrator (the Almighty Ruler of the Universe), which looks down from the domes of Byzantine churches [*279*], combines the forbidding qualities of God the Father with the features of the Son, suggesting Christ's appearance at the *Last Judgment* when he will mete out justice to the living and the dead.

DEËSIS. The image of Christ Enthroned between the Virgin Mary and *St. John the Baptist*, who act as intercessors for mankind, appears so frequently in Byzantine art [*290*, colorplate 15] that it has been given a special name, the Deësis (deh-ee'sis, Gk., supplication). The group also occasionally appears in Western art [*445*] and is a regular feature of depictions of the *Last Judgment* [colorplate 27].

THE VIRGIN AND CHILD. The Virgin Mary with the Christ Child is one of the most common subjects of Christian art and, since many variants of the theme have been developed over the centuries, a number of special designations are regularly used to differentiate the types. In these various images, the Virgin is often called the "Madonna" (It., my lady) even though the work may have been created outside the immediate sphere of Italian art. The type called the "Madonna Enthroned" [*289*] is one of the oldest and emphasizes Mary's position as Queen of Heaven. The motif may be expanded to include attendant angels [*396*, right tympanum; *495*], the prophets who foretold the coming of Christ, and various saints as well [*426, 427, 431*]. This grand, expanded form of the subject, when it appears in Italian art, is sometimes called the "Maestà" (It., majesty). When the figures in a "Madonna and Child with Saints" are shown in a unified spatial setting and converse or join in silent communion with one another, as in Renaissance versions of the subject [colorplate 31, *518, 552*], the picture is called a "Sacra Conversazione" (It., holy conversation). The throne in these images of the seated Virgin establishes her rank as Queen, but when she is shown standing, a type which becomes common in the fourteenth century, she may wear a crown as a symbol of her status [*402, 414*]. About the same time, the Coronation of the Virgin, by Christ, in Heaven, after her death and Assumption, began to be treated as a separate subject [*392*, top; *463*]. Contrasting with the regal images of Mary are those which emphasize her humility, mercy, and motherhood [*549*]. When Mary sits on the ground or on the floor rather than on a throne, she is the "Madonna of Humility;" when she is shown nursing the Christ Child, she is the "Madonna Lactans;" and when she spreads her mantel to shelter a group of the faithful, she is the "Madonna della Misericordia" (It., Madonna of Mercy). When Mary and the infant Jesus are joined by their relatives, St. Joseph (Mary's husband), St. Anne (Mary's mother), or St. Elizabeth (Mary's cousin and the mother of *St. John the Baptist*), the group is known as the "Holy Family" [*468*].

THE FOUR EVANGELISTS. *St. Matthew, St. Mark, St. Luke*, and *St. John*, the authors of the accounts of the life of Jesus known as the four Gospels, are called the Evangelists. They are symbolically represented by a man (Matthew), a lion (Mark), an ox (Luke), and an eagle (John), in accordance with the vision of the four "living creatures" seen by Ezekiel [1: 4–14; colorplate 13, top; *318, 396*, center]. The "beasts" are also used as a means of identifying the "portraits" of the Evangelists [*326, 361*, colorplates 19, 20, *564*]. In church decoration, the surfaces of the four pendentives used to support a dome have been considered appropriate places for portraying the Evangelists or for displaying their symbols [*281, 506*].

THE TWELVE APOSTLES. The traditional list of the twelve disciples of Christ is composed of Peter, Andrew, James, John, Philip, Bartholomew, Matthew, Thomas, James (son of Alphaeus), Jude (or Thaddeus), Simon Zelotes, and Judas Iscariot. These disciples, with the exception of Judas, who betrayed Christ and hanged himself, became the Apostles (fr. Gk. *apostolos*, one sent forth) who preached the gospel throughout the world. St. Matthias was chosen by lot to replace Judas and bring the number of Apostles to twelve (Acts 1: 23–26). In pictures, the number of Apostles is kept at twelve, but it is not always the same twelve who are represented, because more than twelve men came to be called Apostles. *St. Paul* and St. Barnabas, for example, were also called Apostles. In fact, St. Paul is almost always included among the Twelve Apostles in hierarchical and symbolic works or in pictures of those events, occurring after his conversion, such as the "Death of the Virgin" [*399*, colorplate 24] and the *Last Judgment* [colorplate 27], when he might reasonably be expected to be present. Paul is often substituted for St. Jude, and the Evangelists *St. Mark* and *St. Luke* may replace Simon Zelotes and Matthias.

THE FOUR LATIN FATHERS. *St. Jerome*, St. Ambrose, *St. Augustine*, and *St. Gregory* are often grouped together as the Four Latin Fathers, or Doctors, of the Church [*464*]. As scholars, teachers, and interpreters of Scripture, the Fathers are leading representatives of Christ's Church on earth, the Church Militant, and are thus sometimes grouped with the *Four Evangelists*, who represent the Spiritual Church. The Four Greek Fathers are St. John Chrysostom, St. Basil the Great, St. Athanasius, and St. Gregory Nazianzus, but they are seldom represented in Western art. As an ecumenical gesture, Bernini's splendid encasement for the throne of St. Peter in the Vatican [*612*] is borne by two of the Latin Fathers, St. Ambrose and St. Augustine (wearing bishop's mitres), and two of the Greek Fathers, St. Athanasius and St. John Chrysostom.

NARRATIVE SUBJECTS

THE FALL OF MAN

Figures of Adam and Eve [*446, 480, 751*] and the story of their creation [*455*, left; *479, 539*], their disobedience, their censure by the Lord [*285*, bottom; *332*], and their expulsion from the Garden of Eden [colorplate 38, *494*] are common subjects of Christian art, because in the sin of the first man and the first woman all mankind sinned and thus lost the promise of eternal life which was regained only through Christ's sacrifice on the Cross. In serial depictions of the life of Christ, the story of their fall from grace often appears as a necessary prelude, because it explains the necessity of the Incarnation. If only one picture appears, it almost always shows the central act of their disobedience when, tempted by the serpent, Eve ate of the fruit of the Tree of the Knowledge of Good and Evil and gave Adam some of the fruit to eat also (Genesis 3: 1–6). The fruit is not specified in the Bible, but it is usually represented as an *apple*. Adam and Eve are shown reaching for the fruit [colorplate 38, *583*], just holding it, eating it [*285*, bottom left], or covering their nakedness with fig leaves [*263, 285*], since, after having eaten of it, "the eyes of them both were opened, and they knew that they were naked; and they sewed fig leaves together and made themselves aprons" (Genesis 3: 7).

THE INCARNATION

THE ANNUNCIATION. Mankind had lost the gift of eternal life through the sin of Adam and Eve, but Jesus Christ, the second person of the *Trinity*, "for our salvation came down from heaven, and was incarnate by the Holy Ghost of the Virgin Mary: and was made man" (Nicene Creed). Christ, the second Adam, through his sacrifice on the Cross, washed away the sin of the first Adam and regained the gift of eternal life for all mankind. On the day of the Incarnation, when God was made flesh, the Archangel Gabriel appeared to the Virgin Mary and announced that she had been chosen to bear the Son of God (Luke 1: 26–38). In the simplest representations of this "Annunciation," the figures of Gabriel and Mary appear without any indication of setting [*279*, lower left; *352*, lower lêft; *400*, left], although Luke specifically mentions that "the angel came *in* unto her." Mary is often pensive, because when Gabriel appeared he said, "Hail thou that art highly favoured, the Lord is with thee: blessed art thou among women," and Mary "was troubled at his saying, and cast in her mind what manner of salutation this should be." In the more illusionistic depictions of the scene, Mary is shown indoors or in a kind of porch [*438, 444, 447, 497*, colorplates 28, 46, left] and may be represented in an attitude of humility, with her hands crossed on her breast as though saying: "Behold the handmaid of the Lord; be it unto me according to thy word." A *dove* is sometimes shown hovering over her as an indication of the very moment of incarnation through the Holy Ghost. Explanations of the symbols of the purity of the Virgin appearing in depictions of the Annunciation are given in the section on Christian signs and symbols, under *garden, glass, lily,* and *washbasin.*

THE VISITATION. After the *Annunciation,* Mary went to visit her cousin Elizabeth, of whom the Archangel Gabriel had said: ". . . she hath also conceived a son in her old age: and this is the sixth month with her, who was called barren" (Luke 1: 36). The child which Elizabeth bore was *St. John the Baptist* and when "Elizabeth heard the salutation of Mary, the babe leaped in her womb; and Elizabeth was filled with the Holy Ghost: and she spake out with a loud voice, and said, Blessed art thou among women, and blessed is the fruit of thy womb" (Luke 1: 41, 42). Elizabeth is honored as the first to recognize the true identity of Mary's child, because she then said: "And whence is this to me, that the mother of my Lord should come to me?" Elizabeth and Mary are usually easily distinguished in representations of the scene, because Elizabeth is "in her old age" [*352*, bottom right; *400*, right; *453*, left background].

THE NATIVITY. A scene depicting the birth of Christ (Luke 2: 1–7) is known as a "Nativity"; the term is usually reserved for depictions of the Holy Family alone, although angels may be included [*454*] and sometimes two midwives, Zebel and Salome [*412, 413, 443*], in accordance with a legend that Salome doubted the virgin birth and suffered a withered hand.

THE ANNUNCIATION TO THE SHEPHERDS. On the night Christ was born, according to the Gospel of St. Luke (2: 8–14), an angel appeared to shepherds tending their flock and told them of the birth of the Saviour. The subject often appears in the background of representations of the Nativity [*412, 413*]. In paintings, from the fifteenth century on, highly dramatic interpretations may be given the passage: ". . . the glory of the Lord shone round about them: and they were sore afraid" [*443*, background; *453*, background; *454*, background].

THE ADORATION OF THE SHEPHERDS. After the angel had appeared to the shepherds, they went to Bethlehem to see the Christ Child (Luke 2: 15–20): "and they came with haste and found Mary, and Joseph and the babe lying in a manger." The haste of the shepherds is emphasized by Hugo van der Goes in the "Portinari Altarpiece" [Uffizi, *452, 453*]. They are usually shown in an attitude of quiet reverence.

THE ADORATION OF THE MAGI. The Magi were wise men who came from the East to offer gifts to the newborn King of the Jews (Matthew 2: 1–12). They followed the star which had appeared in the heavens with the birth of Christ and had moved before them until it came to rest over Mary and Jesus in Bethlehem [colorplate 26]. Only the Magi and Mary, who holds the Christ Child in her lap, appear in early representations [*352*, center]. There are always three Magi and they came to be represented as kings, offering gifts of gold, frankincense, and myrrh: gold symbolizes the royalty of Christ; frankincense is an emblem of his divinity; and myrrh, a symbol of death, foreshadows his suffering during the Passion. In later representations, the Magi are distinguished according to the ages of man: Caspar, the oldest magus, has a long white beard; Melchior is middle-aged; and Balthasar, who is sometimes represented as a Moor or a negro, is a handsome young man. In International Gothic paintings, they are frequently accompanied by a host of retainers of various ages, dressed in exotic costumes and leading a menagerie of curious beasts. The retinue of the Magi, then, amplifies the significance of the distinctions made among the three kings themselves, who represent the reverence of all nations, all races, and all ages for Christ. The Adoration of the Magi is celebrated, on January 6, by the feast of the Epiphany, the manifestation of Christ to the Gentiles.

THE PRESENTATION IN THE TEMPLE. According to Jewish custom the infant Jesus was brought to Jerusalem by Mary and Joseph who presented him to the Lord in the Temple (Luke 2: 22–39). At the Presentation were St. Simeon, to whom it was promised that "he should not see death, before he had seen the Lord's Christ," and St. Anna the Prophetess, who hailed the Child as the Redeemer [*352,* top; *357,* colorplate 26]. In Melchior Broederlam's "Presentation" [Dijon, *440*], Anna and Simeon are prominent; Simeon, in accordance with the Gospel, takes the Child into his arms; Mary holds a pair of turtledoves with which "to offer a sacrifice according to . . . the law of the Lord." On the western portals at Chartres [*396*], on the second register of the right-hand tympanum, the sacrificial nature of the Presentation is emphasized: the Christ Child is placed directly on the altar, thereby foreshadowing his sacrifice on the Cross.

THE FLIGHT INTO EGYPT. In serial depictions of the life of Christ, the "Presentation in the Temple" is customarily presented immediately after the "Adoration of the Magi." According to St. Matthew (2: 13–18), however, an angel appeared to St. Joseph in a dream, after the Magi had departed, and warned him to take Mary and Jesus and flee into Egypt, because King Herod was about to order the death of all the babies in and around Bethlehem to insure the elimination of the child whom the Magi had called the King of the Jews. In representations of the "Flight" [colorplate 26, bottom center; *606*], Mary is usually shown cradling the Christ Child in her arms while sitting on an ass led by the aged Joseph. Sometimes idols are shown toppling from their pedestals as the Holy Family passes by [*352,* upper left; *440,* right]; sometimes the Holy Family is miraculously nourished in the wilderness; and sometimes they are simply shown resting by the roadside, in which case the subject is known as the "Rest on the Flight into Egypt." When Herod's soldiers are shown killing the babies of Bethlehem, the subject is called the "Massacre of the Innocents."

THE PUBLIC MINISTRY OF CHRIST

THE BAPTISM. After the death of Herod, the Holy Family returned to Israel and settled at Nazareth where Jesus grew to manhood. The beginning of his public ministry is marked by his baptism in the River Jordan by *St. John the Baptist* (Matthew 3: 13–17; Mark 1: 9–11; Luke 3: 21, 22). In representations of the subject [*279,* upper right; *358*], Christ is shown standing in the river as St. John pours the waters over his head and the dove of the Holy Ghost descends from God the Father. Two angels stand on the bank, ready to clothe the naked Christ when he steps from the river.

THE CALLING OF ST. MATTHEW. The drama of Christ's calling of *St. Matthew,* one of the twelve disciples, is heightened by the abruptness of the Gospel accounts (Matthew 9: 9; Mark 2: 14; Luke 5: 27, 28): "And as he passed by, he saw Levi the son of Alphaeus sitting at the receipt of custom, and said unto him, Follow me. And he arose and followed him." Caravaggio [colorplate 49] and Terbrugghen [*631*] make the most of the movement implied in the narrative and translate it into a drama of gestures. St. Matthew, the tax-collector, seated at the counting table, surrounded by misers and spendthrifts, is startled by the sudden appearance of Jesus, who points to Matthew as Matthew questioningly points to himself.

THE SUPPER IN THE HOUSE OF LEVI. Before abandoning everything to follow Jesus, *St. Matthew*, who was also called Levi, "made him a great feast in his own house: and there was a great company of publicans and of others that sat down with them. But their scribes and Pharisees murmured against his disciples, saying, Why do ye eat and drink with publicans and sinners? And Jesus answering said unto them, They that are whole need not a physician; but they that are sick. I came not to call the righteous, but sinners to repentance" (Luke 5: 29–32; also see Matthew 9: 10–13, Mark 2: 15–17). Thus the "buffoons, drunkards, Germans, dwarfs, and similar vulgarities" which Veronese put into the painting [*565*], which the tribunal of the Inquisition at Venice took to be the *Last Supper*, were quite appropriate to the "Supper in the House of Levi," the title which Veronese ultimately assigned the painting to escape a charge of blasphemy.

CHRIST WALKING ON THE WATER. One of the miracles demonstrating the divinity of Christ occurred one night while the disciples, having been sent ahead, were crossing the Sea of Galilee in a boat. In the midst of a storm, which had blown up, Christ came walking to them upon the surface of the waters and when he reached their boat the storm was stilled (Matthew 14: 22–33; Mark 6: 45–52; John 6: 15–21). According to Matthew, *St. Peter* left the boat and attempted to walk to his master over the waves: "But when he saw the wind boisterous, he was afraid; and beginning to sink, he cried, saying, Lord, save me. And immediately Jesus stretched forth his hand, and caught him, and said unto him, O thou of little faith, wherefore didst thou doubt?" When this incident is included, the subject is often called the "Navicella" (L., little ship). The panel by Conrad Witz [Geneva, *457*], which is usually identified as "Christ Walking on the Water," also shows the disciples trying to haul a net full of fish into the boat. When the only disciples shown pulling in the catch are St. Peter, *St. James the Great*, and *St. John the Evangelist*, the subject represented is clearly the "Miraculous Draught of Fishes" (Luke 5: 1–11) after which Peter, James, and John "forsook all" and followed Christ, who told Peter: "Fear not; from henceforth thou shalt catch men." In the painting by Witz, however, seven disciples are present, Peter is in the water, and Jesus, with the weightlessness of an apparition, glides near the shore. All of these elements are in keeping with the account of the appearance of Christ by the Sea of Galilee (also called the "Sea of Tiberias"; John 21) after his *Resurrection*, when a second miraculous draught was made and Peter "did cast himself into the sea."

THE DELIVERY OF THE KEYS TO ST. PETER. In giving *St. Peter* the authority to lead the Church, Christ said: "I will give unto thee the keys of the kingdom of heaven: and whatsoever thou shalt bind on earth shall be bound in heaven: and whatsoever thou shalt loose on earth shall be loosed in heaven" (Matthew 16: 19). In the scriptural account, Christ only speaks metaphorically, but the "Delivery of the Keys" is sometimes depicted as an actual event [*520*] emblematic of papal authority, which is believed to have descended directly from St. Peter, the first pope.

THE TRANSFIGURATION. Perhaps the most dramatic revelation of the divinity of Christ before his *Resurrection* is his "Transfiguration" (Matthew 17: 1–13; Mark 9: 2–13; Luke 9: 28–36) when, after the first missionary journey of the twelve disciples, he took "Peter, James, and John his brother, and bringeth them up into an high mountain apart, and was transfigured before them: and his face did shine as the sun, and his raiment was white as the light. And, behold, there appeared unto them Moses and Elias talking with him" (Matthew 17: 1–3). In the apse mosaic at S. Apollinare in Classe [colorplate 13], the subject is presented in a very elliptical fashion. Christ is represented by a large golden cross, perhaps because Moses and Elijah (Elias) "spake of his decease which he should accomplish at Jerusalem" (Luke 9: 31); Christ's head appears in a medallion at the intersection of the arms of the cross. The three disciples are represented as three *lambs* and Moses and Elijah, who stand for the Law and the prophecies of the Old Testament, which were fulfilled in Christ, are represented as bust-length figures, miraculously emerging from the vari-colored clouds of a sunset sky. The Hand of God, emerging from the clouds at the apex of the apse, is a visual sign of the voice of God: "And there was a cloud that overshadowed them: and a voice came out of the cloud, saying, This is my beloved Son: hear him" (Mark 9: 7). A more literal interpretation of the scene appears in a mosaic covering one of the corners of the nave of the monastery church at Daphne, Greece [*279*, upper left]. The most famous version of the subject is the painting by Raphael in the Vatican.

THE TRIBUTE MONEY. One of Masaccio's well-known frescoes in the Brancacci Chapel [*493*] depicts a story told in the Gospel of St. Matthew (17: 24–27). When a collector of tribute came to *St. Peter* and asked if his master paid tribute, Jesus told Peter: ". . . lest we should offend them, go thou to the sea, and cast an hook, and take up the fish that first cometh up; and when thou hast opened his mouth, thou shalt find a piece of money: that take, and give unto them for me and thee." On a later occasion (Matthew 22: 15–22; Mark 12: 13–17; Luke 20: 19–26), when the spies of the chief priests and scribes tried to trick Jesus into open sedition by asking whether or not it was lawful to give tribute to the Roman emperor, he took a coin and asked them whose image it bore. When they answered, "Caesar's," Jesus said, "Render therefore unto Caesar the things which be Caesar's, and unto God the things which be God's" (Luke 20: 25).

THE PARABLE OF THE PRODIGAL SON. Although pictures which simply show Christ preaching [*640*] are not common, many of the parables, which he used as vivid examples of moral or immoral behavior, have been literally depicted as actual events. Among the most popular is the parable of the Prodigal Son (Luke 15: 11–32), which typifies the central Christian concept of Repentance and forgiveness [*639*]. The Prodigal, having asked for his share of the family goods, "wasted his substance with riotous living," but on his return to his father's house, "his father saw him, and had compassion, and ran, and fell on his neck, and kissed him. And the son said unto him, Father, I have sinned against heaven, and in thy sight, and am no more worthy to be called thy son. But the father said to his servants, Bring forth the best robe, and put it on him; and put a ring on his hand, and shoes on his feet: and bring hither the fatted calf, and kill it; and let us eat, and be merry: for this my son was dead, and is alive again; he was lost, and is found."

THE PASSION

THE ENTRY INTO JERUSALEM. Serial depictions of the Passion (the sufferings of Christ during the last days of his earthly life) often begin joyfully with his triumphal entry into Jerusalem [*263*, center of lower register; colorplate 22, *428*; Matthew 21: 1–11, Mark 11: 1–11, Luke 19: 28–44, John 12: 12–19]. When Christ and his disciples were just outside Jerusalem, at the Mount of Olives, he sent two of them to fetch an ass and her colt. This was done to fulfill the prophecy of Zechariah: "Tell ye the daughter of Sion, Behold, thy King cometh unto thee, meek, and sitting upon an ass, and a colt the foal of an ass. And the disciples went, and did as Jesus commanded them, and brought the ass, and the colt, and put on them their clothes, and they set him thereon. And a very great multitude spread their garments in the way; others cut down branches from the trees, and strawed them in the way. And the multitudes that went before, and that followed, cried, saying, Hosanna to the son of David: Blessed is he that cometh in the name of the Lord; Hosanna in the highest" (Matthew 21: 5–9). This scene is usually set just outside one of the gates to Jerusalem and is depicted much as it is described in the Gospels. In Giotto's fresco in the Arena Chapel [colorplate 22] even the mouths of the multitudes are opened wide as they cry, "Hosanna!" The man looking down from the branches of a tree is a traditional feature of the scene which is probably borrowed from a slightly earlier episode described by St. Luke (19: 1–6). As Jesus was passing through Jericho on his way to Jerusalem, Zacchaeus, a rich publican (tax-collector), who "was little of stature," ran before Jesus and "climbed up into a sycamore tree to see him: for he was to pass that way. And when Jesus came to the place, he looked up, and saw him, and said unto him, Zacchaeus, make haste, and come down; for today I must abide at thy house."

THE LAST SUPPER. The Passover meal, which was the last Christ was to eat together with his disciples (Matthew 26: 17–30; Mark 14: 12–26; Luke 22: 7–38), is usually represented either at the moment of the institution of the Eucharist (the Sacrament of Holy Communion) or at the moment of Christ's announcement that one among those present at the table would betray him. In representations of the latter type, it was customary, before Leonardo painted his famous version of the subject in Milan [*524*], to isolate Judas Iscariot, the betrayer, alone on one side of the table [*499*]. In Leonardo's painting, as in earlier examples, the disciples are shown reacting variously to the words: "Verily I say unto you, that one of you shall betray me." But the youthful *St. John*, who is usually shown drowsily leaning against Jesus (John 13: 25) or with his head on the table, leans away from Jesus. John's silhouette forms the edge of one of the two great wave-like movements to either side of Christ, who is a still point in a storm of emotions. Although the gesturing figures in Tintoretto's "Last Supper" at S. Giorgio Maggiore, Venice [*559*], are even more turbulent than Leonardo's, the artist stresses the sacramental nature of the subject rather than the drama of betrayal. This was appropriate at a time, during the Counter Reformation, when the doctrine of transubstantiation (the transformation of the bread and wine of the Eucharist into the very substance of the body and blood of Christ) was under sharp attack by the Protestants. Tintoretto, or his patrons, chose to present the moment when Christ "took bread, and gave thanks, and brake it, and gave unto them, saying, This is my body which is given for you: this do in remembrance of me" (Luke 22: 19).

CHRIST WASHING THE FEET OF THE DISCIPLES. According to the Gospel of St. John (13: 1–17), Christ rose from the table after eating the Last Supper with his twelve disciples and, as an example of humility, washed their feet: "If I then, your Lord and Master, have washed your feet; ye also ought to wash one another's feet . . . Verily, verily, I say unto you, The servant is not greater than his lord; neither he that is sent greater than he that sent him." When he came to *St. Peter*—the moment usually chosen for representing the subject [colorplate 19]—Peter protested, saying: "Thou shalt never wash my feet. Jesus answered him, If I wash thee not, thou hast no part with me. Simon Peter saith unto him, Lord, not my feet only, but also my hands and my head. Jesus saith to him, He that is washed needeth not save to wash his feet, but is clean every whit: and ye are clean, but not all. For he knew who should betray him; therefore said he, Ye are not all clean."

THE AGONY IN THE GARDEN. Leaving the upper room in the house where they ate the *Last Supper*, Jesus and his disciples went beyond the walls of Jerusalem to a garden called Gethsemane (Matthew 26: 36–46; Mark 14: 32–42; Luke 22: 39–46). Taking *St. Peter*, *St. James*, and *St. John* apart with him, he said: "My soul is exceeding sorrowful, even unto death: tarry ye here, and watch with me. And he went a little farther, and fell on his face, and prayed, saying, O my Father, if it be possible, let this cup pass from me: nevertheless not as I will, but as thou wilt" (Matthew 26: 38–39). In representations of the subject, the cup of suffering is shown physically present in the form of a Eucharistic chalice. Sometimes, it is held by the angel mentioned by St. Luke (22: 43, 44): "And there appeared an angel unto him from heaven, strengthening him. And being in an agony he prayed more earnestly: and his sweat was as it were great drops of blood falling down to the ground." Peter, James, and John are usually shown near Jesus, but they are sound asleep. In the accounts in Matthew and Mark, Jesus wakes Peter and asks: "What, could ye not watch with me one hour? Watch and pray, that ye enter not into temptation: the spirit indeed is willing, but the flesh is weak" (Matthew 26: 40, 41). Returning to the three disciples a second time, Jesus again finds all three asleep and, after leaving to pray again, returns and finally says: "Sleep on now, and take your rest: behold the hour is at hand, and the Son of man is betrayed into the hands of sinners" (Matthew 26: 45). The praying Christ, the chalice, and the three sleeping disciples can be seen at the start of the Passion series painted around the mirror in the background of Jan van Eyck's Portrait of Giovanni Arnolfini and his bride [*450*, bottom].

THE BETRAYAL. Immediately after Christ's *Agony in the Garden*, when it was still dark, Judas came to the garden of Gethsemane with "a great multitude with swords and staves, from the chief priests and the elders of the people. Now he that betrayed him gave them a sign, saying, Whomsoever I shall kiss, that same is he: hold him fast. And forthwith he came to Jesus, and said, Hail, master; and kissed him. And Jesus said unto him, Friend, wherefore art thou come? Then came they, and laid hands on Jesus, and took him" (Matthew 26: 47–50; cf. Mark 14: 43–52, Luke 22: 47–54, John 18: 1–13). *St. Peter* attempted to defend his master and struck out with his sword, cutting off the ear of Malchus, a servant of the high priest [*406*], but Jesus said: "Put up thy sword into the sheath: the cup which my Father hath given me, shall I not drink it?" (John 18: 11).

THE DENIAL OF PETER. *St. Peter*, keeping at a distance, followed the band of men that took Jesus to the palace of Caiaphas, the high priest. He entered the palace and sat with the servants while, in another part of the building, Christ was being charged with blasphemy. As Peter was warming himself by the fire, one of the maids accused him of being a follower of Jesus, but Peter denied it. Two others also came and accused him of knowing Jesus. "Then began he to curse and to swear, saying, I know not the man. And immediately the cock crew. And Peter remembered the word of Jesus, which said unto him, Before the cock crow, thou shalt deny me thrice. And he went out, and wept bitterly" (Matthew 26: 74, 75; also see Mark 14: 54, 66–72, Luke 22: 54–62, John 18: 15–18, 25–27). On the choir screen at Naumburg Cathedral [*405*], just to the left of the gable over the entrance to the choir, Peter is shown shrinking from the accusing hand of the maid of the high priest.

CHRIST BEFORE PILATE. The morning after Christ was accused of blasphemy before Caiaphas, the high priest, he was taken before Pontius Pilate, the Roman governor of Judea, and charged with treason for calling himself "King of the Jews" (Matthew 27: 11–26, Mark 15: 1–15, Luke 23: 1–7, 13–25, John 18: 28–40, 19: 4–16). After a preliminary examination by Pilate, Jesus, according to St. Luke (23: 8–11), was sent for judgment to Herod Antipas, governor of Galilee, who was in Jerusalem for the Passover, but the subject is seldom represented. Herod's soldiers mocked Jesus, arraying him in a "gorgeous robe," and then returned him to Pilate, who presented him to the multitude and offered to release him as the prisoner who, according to custom, the governor was to free each year during Passover. But the mob, stirred up by the priests, cried out for the release of Barabbas, a murderer, and demanded that Jesus be crucified. Whereupon, Pilate "washed his hands before the multitude, saying, I am innocent of the blood of this just person: see ye to it" (Matthew 27: 24). This is the moment usually chosen for representing Christ's appearance before Pilate [*263*, upper right; colorplate 44]. Pilate again appears with Jesus in the subject which is called the "Ecce Homo" (Behold the man) after his words to the multitude during a second appeal for their sympathy, after Christ had been scourged and mocked (John 19: 4–7).

THE FLAGELLATION. After the mob cried out for the release of Barabbas instead of Christ, Pilate had his soldiers take Jesus away to be scourged and crucified (Matthew 27: 26, Mark 15: 15, John 19: 1). The "Flagellation" (or "Scourging") of Christ, although only mentioned in passing by the Evangelists, is usually fully treated as a separate scene in serial representations of the Passion. Christ, naked except for a loin cloth, is usually shown bound to a column while he is being lashed by two men, each holding a cat-o'-nine-tails or a bundle of switches [*450*, left].

CHRIST CROWNED WITH THORNS. Unlike the *Flagellation*, the "Mocking of Christ" by the soldiers of Pilate [*555*]—also called "Christ Crowned with Thorns"—is described in considerable detail by the Evangelists: "Then the soldiers of the governor took Jesus into the common hall, and gathered unto him the whole band of soldiers. And they stripped him, and put on him a scarlet robe. And when they had platted a crown of thorns, they put it upon his head, and a reed in his right hand: and they bowed the knee before him, and mocked him, saying, Hail, King of the Jews! And they spit upon him, and took the reed, and smote him on the head" (Matthew 27: 27–30; cf. Mark 15: 16–19, John 19: 1–3). Although it is the mocking of Christ by the soldiers of Pilate that is most frequently portrayed, he had already been mocked twice before: first, in the palace of Caiaphas, the high priest (Matthew 26: 67–68, Mark 14: 65, Luke 22: 63–65), and, second, when he was brought before Herod Antipas (Luke 23: 11), a subject which is seldom represented, probably because it includes no action not described at greater length in the other accounts. The mocking of Christ before Caiaphas is easily distinguished from his mocking by the soldiers of Pilate, because Christ does not wear a crown of thorns and is shown blindfolded while men hit him saying, "Prophesy unto us, thou Christ, Who is he that smote thee?" (Matthew 26: 68).

THE BEARING OF THE CROSS. Of the Gospel accounts of the "Road to Calvary" (Via Crucis), only John (19: 17) states that Christ carried his cross himself; the other Evangelists say that a passerby, Simon of Cyrene, was compelled to carry his cross for him (Matthew 27: 32, Mark 15: 21, Luke 23: 26), but in most depictions of the subject, Christ himself struggles beneath the weight of the cross [*450*, upper left], although Simon is often present and may assist him [colorplate 23]. Often, the "great company of people, and of women, which also bewailed and lamented him" (Luke 23: 27) are shown issuing from the city gate through which, only a few days before, Christ had entered in triumph. St. Luke (23: 27–31) recounts Christ's admonition to the "Daughters of Jerusalem," but the Gospel accounts are bare compared to the wealth of incident with which legend has enriched the Via Crucis. Many of the legendary incidents which appear in paintings and reliefs stem from the popular devotion known as the "Stations of the Cross," which was developed by the Franciscans. The fourteen "stations" or scenes are: (1) Jesus condemned to death; (2) Jesus taking up his cross; (3) Jesus falling for the first time beneath the cross; (4) Jesus meeting his sorrowing mother; (5) Simon of Cyrene compelled to help Jesus carry the cross; (6) St. Veronica wiping the face of Jesus with her veil (sudarium), which miraculously retained his likeness; (7) Jesus falling the second time; (8) Jesus admonishing the Daughters of Jerusalem; (9) Jesus falling the third time; (10) Jesus stripped of his garments; (11) Jesus nailed to the cross; (12) Jesus dying on the cross; (13) the descent from the cross; (14) the entombment.

THE CRUCIFIXION. Early representations of the Crucifixion are essentially symbolic or devotional rather than historical in character. Instead of showing the subject as it might have appeared to a spectator at a particular moment and from a particular viewpoint [colorplate 27], artists stressed the timeless significance of the sacrifice by which all mankind was redeemed. No attempt was made to include the wealth of detail which is implied by the descriptions in the Gospels (Matthew 27: 33–56, Mark 15: 22–41, Luke 23: 32–49, John 19: 17–37). In fact, the Crucifixion may be represented by no more than a crucifix, showing only the body (called the "corpus") on the cross [*328*]. Mourning angels, swooping and diving in their grief, and weeping personifications of the sun and moon may be added as an expression of cosmic woe [colorplate 18; cf. Luke 23: 44, 45], but the Virgin Mary, on Christ's right, and *St. John the Evangelist*, on his left, are often the only mortals present [*284, 405, 450* top; see John 19: 26, 27]. One early type of Crucifixion shows Christ on the cross flanked by two soldiers [*317*], one holding the reed topped by the vinegar-soaked *sponge* from which Christ drank (Matthew 27: 48) and the other (traditionally, St. Longinus) holding the spear with which he pierced Christ's side (John 19 :34). This group may be expanded by the addition of Mary and John to either side. In these early representations of the Crucifixion, Christ is nailed to the cross with four nails [*284, 317*, colorplate 18], but, beginning in the thirteenth century, three nails become customary: one through each hand and one piercing both feet [*405*, colorplate 27, *579*]. This permitted the artist to dispose the limbs of the corpus either more gracefully or in a more anguished position than is possible if each foot is nailed separately. The *skull*, which sometimes appears at the base of the cross [*284, 411*, colorplate 29], marks the place of crucifixion as Golgotha ("the place of a skull"), according to tradition, the very spot where Adam was buried. The skull, then, is the very skull of Adam, whose sin is washed away by the blood trickling from the wounds of Christ.

THE DESCENT FROM THE CROSS. Matthew (27: 57–59), Mark (15: 42–46), Luke (23: 50–53), and John (19: 38–40) all recount how Joseph of Arimathaea, a rich counsellor and a follower of Christ, begged the body of Jesus from Pilate, took it down from the cross, and wrapped it in fine linen. John, alone, mentions Nicodemus, who brought a mixture of myrrh and aloes and helped Joseph wind the body "in linen clothes with the spices, as the manner of the Jews is to bury." Only Joseph of Arimathaea and Nicodemus, then, are specifically mentioned in the Gospels as being present during the "Descent from the Cross" (or "Deposition" as it is sometimes called), but, in representations of the subject [colorplates 29, 42], the Virgin Mary, *St. John the Evangelist, St. Mary Magdalene*, and a few disciples are usually included as well. Joseph of Arimathaea, the rich counsellor, is usually older than Nicodemus, whose attribute is the jar of spices which he brought.

THE PIETÀ. The image of the sorrowing Virgin holding the dead Christ [*408, 437, 460, 548*] is usually known by the Italian word *Pietà* (literally, "pity," fr. L. *pietas*, piety), although it was a type of devotional image (*Andachtsbild*) first developed in Northern Europe. An expanded version of the subject, with a number of additional figures such as *St. John, St. Mary Magdalene*, Joseph of Arimathaea, Nicodemus, and the disciples, is usually known as the "Lamentation" [*430*] instead of the *Pietà*. Both types are artistic inventions which have no specific basis in Scripture.

THE ENTOMBMENT. The actual burial of the body of Christ, as distinct from the Lamentation over the body, is known as the "Entombment" [*450, right*], Joseph of Arimathaea and Nicodemus are usually shown lowering the body by means of the linen winding sheet mentioned by all four Evangelists. The Virgin, *St. Mary Magdalene, St. John*, and other disciples may assist or look on. St. Luke (23: 55) mentions specifically that the "women also, which came with him from Galilee, followed after, and beheld the sepulchre, and how his body was laid." While St. John (19: 41) states that the sepulchre was in a garden in the very place where Christ was crucified. According to Matthew and Mark, when Joseph had laid the body in the sepulchre, which is described as Joseph's "own new tomb, which he had hewn out in the rock," he "rolled a great stone to the door of the sepulchre, and departed" (Matthew 27: 60). The sepulchre, which is clearly described as a cave hewn out of a large outcropping of rock (Mark 15: 46), is not often represented in medieval and Renaissance Entombments; the body is usually shown being lowered into a conventional rectangular sarcophagus without any suggestion of the rock-hewn sepulchre and its great stone door.

THE DESCENT INTO LIMBO. It is a point of Christian doctrine that, in the interval between the *Entombment* and the *Resurrection*, Christ descended into Hell, although the event is not actually described in the canonical books of the Bible, but in the apochryphal "Gospel of Nicodemus, or the Acts of Pilate." The "Descent" is sometimes called the "Harrowing of Hell" and Christ is sometimes shown freeing souls from the very jaws of Hell [*450, right*], but it is generally believed that the place to which he descended was not the region of the eternally damned, nor even Purgatory, but a special place called Limbo, the abode of the souls of those good people who awaited the Redemption of man's sins (through Christ's sacrifice on the Cross) before they could be admitted to Heaven. Prominent among the patriarchs and prophets of the Old Testament, whom Christ frees, are Adam and Eve, whose sin made Christ's sacrifice necessary. Christ usually carries the triumphal banner of the Cross [*755*] and is sometimes shown trapping Satan beneath the prison gates which he has just battered down [*286*].

THE RESURRECTION. The moment of the actual Resurrection of Christ from his tomb is not directly described in the Bible, but it often appears as a triumphant conclusion to serial presentations of the Passion [*450, lower right*]. As proof of the bodily Resurrection, the soldiers, whom the priests and Pharisees had requested from Pilate to keep watch on the tomb (Matthew 27: 62–66), are shown sprawled on the ground while Christ steps out of a sarcophagus or hovers weightlessly above it [colorplate 46]. The motif of the sleeping or falling soldiers is taken from the description by St. Matthew (28: 1–8) of the appearance of the angel of the Lord to *St. Mary Magdalene* and Mary, the mother of James, on Easter morning: "And behold, there was a great earthquake: for the angel of the Lord descended from heaven, and came and rolled back the stone from the door, and sat upon it . . . And for fear of him the keepers did shake, and became as dead men."

THE ASCENSION. During the forty days between his *Resurrection* on Easter morning and his Ascension into Heaven, Christ appeared several times to his followers. His first appearance, to *St. Mary Magdalene* (Mark 16: 9–10, John 20: 11–18), is known in art as the "Noli me tangere" (Touch me not), because of his injunction to Mary, at the time, not to touch him because he had not yet ascended to his Father. Another appearance, which is sometimes represented, was to two of his disciples on the road to Emmaus (Luke 24: 13–29) after which he broke bread with them during the "Supper at Emmaus" (Luke 24: 30–35). Christ also appeared to *St. Thomas*, who doubted the truth of his bodily resurrection, and allowed him to thrust his finger into the wound in his side (John 20: 24–29), a subject known as the "Incredulity of Thomas." Christ's final appearance to the disciples was at his Ascension, which is described by St. Luke, in his Gospel (24: 50–53) and in the Acts of the Apostles: ". . . while they beheld, he was taken up; and a cloud received him out of their sight. And while they looked stedfastly toward heaven as he went up, behold, two men stood by them in white apparel; which also said, Ye men of Galilee, why stand ye gazing up into heaven? this same Jesus, which is taken up from you into heaven, shall so come in like manner as ye have seen him go into heaven" (Acts 1: 9–11) [cf. *396*, left tympanum].

THE MISSION OF THE APOSTLES AND THE SECOND COMING

PENTECOST. Ten days after the *Ascension* of Christ, on the day of the Jewish harvest festival of Pentecost, when the Apostles were gathered together, "suddenly there came a sound from heaven as of a rushing mighty wind, and it filled all the house where they were sitting. And there appeared unto them cloven tongues like as of fire, and it sat upon each of them. And they were all filled with the Holy Ghost, and began to speak with other tongues, as the Spirit gave them utterance" (Acts 2: 2–4). This "Descent of the Holy Ghost upon the Apostles," or "Pentecost" as the subject is also called, marks the beginning of the mission of the Apostles to spread the gospel throughout the earth (hence, the gift of tongues). An unusual version of the subject is found at Vézelay [*354*], where Christ appears in a *mandorla*, with rays spreading from his fingers to the heads of the Apostles; ordinarily, small tongues of flame are shown hovering over the heads of the Apostles. The Virgin and others are also often included and the *Dove* of the Holy Ghost usually represents the Godhead rather than the figure of Christ, as at Vézelay.

THE LAST JUDGMENT. The Second Coming of Christ at the end of the world, when he shall come in glory "to judge both the living and the dead," is part of the Nicene Creed, the "Credo" of the Mass, but it is not fully developed as a subject for art until the Romanesque period when it appears carved on a large scale on the tympana of the portals of churches [*353*]. There is no single Biblical text which served as a source for artists; rather, the image was formed from parts of the many references and descriptions of the day of judgment which are scattered throughout the Bible. In its complex late Gothic form, the subject is divided into several zones [colorplate 27]. In the zone of Heaven, Christ appears in glory, displaying the wounds of the crucifixion as a sign of his right to judge (cf. Revelation 1: 7). He is surrounded by angels (Mark 13: 26, 27), some of whom bear the *Instruments of the Passion* and some of whom blow trumpets to wake the dead (I Corinthians 15: 52). To either side of Christ, the Virgin Mary and *St. John the Baptist* kneel as intercessors for mankind. The twelve Apostles (Luke 22: 30) and a host of the saints (I Corinthians 6: 2) fill the rest of the heavenly zone about the figure of Christ [*540*]. Depending on the format of the picture, the naked souls who have been saved and are welcomed to Heaven and clothed by *St. Peter* and the angels, may also be included near Christ. *St. Michael* (Daniel 12: 1), in full armor and carrying the scales of justice, may serve as a transitional figure between the zone of Heaven and the zone of Earth, where the naked figures of the dead rise from their graves (Daniel 12: 2). Those who were lost or buried at sea may also be shown rising from their watery graves (Revelation 20: 13). The just rise toward Heaven but the damned fall into the zone of Hell, where they are tormented by demons [*416, 538*]. The Last Judgment should not be confused with another subject commonly carved on the tympana of church portals: the Apocalyptic vision of the throne of God (Revelation 4), in which Christ, enclosed by a *mandorla*, appears with the four symbols of the Evangelists and the "four and twenty elders."

OLD TESTAMENT PREFIGURATIONS OF NEW TESTAMENT EVENTS

Events of the Old Testament are frequently represented in Christian art because they were thought to foreshadow, or prefigure, the events of the New Testament. Beneath the literal meaning of the Biblical narrative was found a mystical, or "anagogical," meaning relating to the life of Christ. Scripture was searched for corresponding passages and the most tenuous parallels were drawn to construct a system of Old Testament "types" and New Testament "antitypes." Moses, David, Job and many others were interpreted as types of Christ and the various circumstances of their lives were seen as "figures" of incidents recounted in the Gospels. A few of the more common types and figures are explained below.

ABEL'S SACRIFICE. Cain and Abel, the sons of Adam and Eve, both offered sacrifices to the Lord (Genesis 4: 3–7). Cain, who "brought of the fruit of the ground," is shown with a sheaf of grain and Abel, who was a "keeper of sheep" and "brought of the firstlings of his flock," is shown offering a lamb [*446*, top]. The Lord, "who had respect unto Abel and his offering," is sometimes represented by a large hand reaching out of the clouds toward Abel's lamb [*356*, bottom]. Medieval commentators linked Abel and his lamb with Jesus, the Lamb of God, who sacrificed himself to redeem mankind.

CAIN KILLING ABEL. The Lord accepted Abel's sacrifice, "but unto Cain and to his offering he had not respect. And Cain was very wroth, and his countenance fell" and, out of envy, he "rose up against Abel his brother, and slew him" (Genesis 4: 8). This was the first murder, clear evidence of the sin of man which was washed away by the blood of Christ the Lamb [*445, 446*, top]. Abel, killed by his brother Cain, was seen as a type of Christ betrayed by Judas.

MELCHIZEDEK OFFERING ABRAHAM BREAD AND WINE. When Abraham returned from his victory over the kings who had sacked Sodom and captured his nephew Lot, "Melchizedek king of Salem brought forth bread and wine: and he was the priest of the most high God" (Genesis 14: 18). The author of the Epistle to the Hebrews (Chapter 7) compares the priesthood of Melchizedek to the priesthood of Christ who "offered up himself." Commentators developed the analogy, pointing out the kingship as well as the priesthood of both Melchizedek and Christ and interpreting the offering of bread and wine to Abraham as a prefiguration of the institution of the Eucharist. In the carving of the subject at Reims [*401*], Melchizedek, in fact, holds a Eucharistic chalice in one hand and offers Abraham a consecrated wafer with the other.

ABRAHAM'S SACRIFICE OF ISAAC. Among the prefigurations which frequently accompany representations of the Crucifixion in medieval art, the "Sacrifice of Isaac" (Genesis 22: 1–19) is the most common [*263*, upper left; *419*]. Analogies were drawn between Abraham's willingness to sacrifice his beloved only son, Isaac, and God the Father's sacrifice of his Son, Jesus. Isaac carrying the wood to the sacrifice was seen as a type of Christ Bearing the Cross and the "ram caught in a thicket by his horns," which Abraham sacrificed in place of his son, was taken as an allusion to Christ's crown of thorns. The two horns of the ram were interpreted as a symbol of the two arms of the Cross. In Early Christian art, as on the sarcophagus of Junius Bassus [Vatican, *263*], the allusion to Christ's sacrifice was made more pointed by substituting a *lamb* for the ram.

JACOB WRESTLING WITH THE ANGEL. One night, during his journey to meet his brother Esau, Jacob wrestled until daybreak with an angel and "touched the hollow of his thigh," refusing to release him until he had received the angel's blessing [Genesis 32: 24–32; *262*, colorplate 69]. "And Jacob called the name of the place Peniel [face of God]: for I have seen God face to face, and my life is preserved." This was interpreted as a figure of the "Incredulity of St. Thomas" (John 20: 24–29), because Thomas touched the wound in the side of the risen Christ as Jacob touched the hollow of the angel's thigh.

JACOB BLESSING THE SONS OF JOSEPH. Joseph took his sons, Manasseh and Ephraim, who were born in Egypt, to be blessed by his dying father Jacob (Genesis 48). In blessing his grandsons, Jacob (or Israel, as he was called after wrestling with the angel at Peniel) crossed his arms, laying his right hand on Ephraim's head and his left on Manasseh's [colorplate 52]. The crossing of Jacob's arms was seen as a figure of the Cross. The special favor shown Ephraim, who was blessed with Jacob's right hand, although he was the younger of the two brothers, was interpreted as a sign of the supplanting of the Old Covenant by the New, through Christ's sacrifice on the Cross. Thus, Manasseh represents the Jews, and Ephraim, the younger brother, symbolizes the Christians who replaced the "chosen people" in God's favor.

THE CROSSING OF THE RED SEA. The miraculous passage of the Israelites through the Red Sea and the drowning of the pursuing Egyptians [Exodus 14: 21–31; *365*], not only appears as an example of salvation through divine intervention but, more abstrusely, as a type of the *Baptism* of Christ. Moses [*410, 535*], who led the Israelites out of Egypt and brought them God's commandments from Sinai, represents the Old Law and is the chief type of Christ, who brought the New.

DAVID AND GOLIATH. David's victory over Goliath, the prideful Philistine giant [I Samuel 17: 38–54; *425, 481, 500, 534, 609*], was understood as a prefiguration of Christ's triumph over the Devil through his sacrifice on the Cross. As David saved the Israelites from Goliath and the Philistines, so Christ saved the souls in Limbo from the prideful power of the Devil and his demons [*286*].

THE MISERY OF JOB. The story of Job, the upright and God-fearing man of the land of Uz, whom God allowed to suffer at the hands of Satan, was seen as an allegory of the Passion of Christ. Job, as Christ, triumphed over the Devil and, after a period of profound anguish, was restored to a position of honor, receiving "twice as much as he had before" (Job 42: 10). On the sarcophagus of Junius Bassus [Vatican, *263*, lower left], Job's wife stands off from her debased and diseased husband, covering her nose and mouth, as she offers him food on a stick.

JONAH AND THE WHALE. The miraculous delivery of Jonah from the belly of the "great fish" which "vomited out Jonah upon the dry land" [Jonah 2; *252*], like Daniel's delivery from death in the lion's den [Daniel 6: 16–23; *263*, lower right], was a common Early Christian emblem of the certainty of salvation for those who had faith in the Lord. Christ himself, however, lent a deeper significance to the story by drawing an analogy with his own coming death and resurrection: "Even as Jonah was three days and three nights in the belly of the whale, so shall the Son of man be three days and three nights in the depths of the earth" (Matthew 12: 40).

CHAPTER FOUR

SAINTS AND THEIR ATTRIBUTES

ST. AGNES (*It.* Agnese, *Fr.* Agnès, *Sp.* Inez), d. c. 304, beautiful, young virgin martyr, patroness of maidens, who chose dishonor and death rather than desert Christ, her spiritual lover, for the pagan son of a prefect of Rome. Stripped naked by order of the prefect, she was led to a brothel on the site of Borromini's S. Agnese [*619*], on the Piazza Navona in Rome, but her hair suddenly grew so long that it covered her shame. In commemoration of this miracle, she is often represented with long tresses. Sometimes, she is shown with a sword, the instrument of her martyrdom, but her special attribute is the lamb (*agnus*), a punning reference to her name, and sign of her meekness and innocence. She is represented holding her lamb on Duccio's "Maestà" altarpiece and on the Ghent Altarpiece [*445*], where she appears in the forefront of the company of virgin martyrs.

ST. ANTHONY ABBOT (*It.* Antonio, *Fr.* Antoine, *Sp.* Antonio, *Ger.* Antonius), c. 251–356, Egyptian hermit, venerated as the founder of monasticism. As a young man, he renounced the world, divided his wealth among the poor, and went into the desert where he led a solitary and ascetic life. In his solitude, he was tempted by demons, who, despairing of corrupting him with lures of the flesh, fell on him and beat him senseless [*467*]. Anthony is represented as an old man with a long, white beard; he is dressed in the habit of a monk, which is often marked with a blue letter T (for "Theos," God), as in the Ghent Altarpiece [*445*] where he leads the group of Holy Hermits. He is usually shown resting his aged bones on a rustic crutch and carrying a bell with which to exorcize demons [*452*]. St. Anthony Abbot should not be confused with St. Anthony of Padua, who lived in the thirteenth century, and was famous for his preaching and his miracles. St. Anthony of Padua is represented as a young Franciscan monk and is often shown carrying a lily and holding the Christ Child.

ST. AUGUSTINE (*It*. Agostino, *Fr*. Augustin, *Sp*. Augustino, *Ger*. Augustinus), 354–430, one of the Four Latin Fathers of the Church (Augustine, Ambrose, *Jerome*, and *Gregory*). After the profligate youth and the long period of spiritual turmoil described in his "Confessions," Augustine embraced Christianity and was baptized by St. Ambrose in Milan, where he had settled as a teacher of rhetoric. Returning to his native North Africa, he became a priest and was appointed bishop of Hippo, where he died during a siege of the city by the Vandals. The brilliance of his theological writings, the most famous of which is the "City of God," has assured his veneration as patron saint of theologians and scholars. St. Augustine is usually shown wearing the mitre and vestments of a bishop [colorplate 45]; often, he holds one of his many books [*612*]. The little child with the spoon, shown at his feet in Michael Pacher's "Altarpiece of the Four Latin Fathers" [Munich, *464*], is a reference to a vision he had while writing his discourse on the Trinity. Walking along the seashore, he came upon a child who told him that he was trying to pour all the water of the sea into a hole which he had dug in the sand. When Augustine told him that it was impossible, the child replied, "Not more impossible than for thee, Oh Augustine, to explain the mystery on which thou art now meditating."

ST. BARBARA (*Fr*. Barbe), third century?, one of the most popular virgin saints, protectress against fire, lightning, and sudden death. Barbara's special attribute is a tower, which appears behind her in a landscape or is held, as a model, in her hand. The tower is an allusion to the legend that she was shut up in a high tower at Heliopolis in Egypt by her pagan father, Dioscorus, who loved her so much that he wished to keep her from the sight of men. Visited by a disciple of Origen, who disguised himself as a physician, she was converted and baptized. Often, as in the Ghent Altarpiece [*445*], where Barbara, holding her attribute, appears with *St. Agnes* in the forefront of the group of Holy Virgins, the tower is pierced with precisely three windows. This is in reference to the third window which Barbara told workmen to insert into the splendid bath-chamber which her doting father had ordered to be built for her. When questioned by Dioscorus about the extra window, Barbara answered: "Know, my father, that through three windows doth the soul receive light—the Father, the Son, and the Holy Ghost; and the Three are One." She thus betrayed her new faith and Dioscorus, faithful to the old gods, turned upon his daughter and, when she refused to recant, beheaded her. For this unnatural act he was consumed in a sudden crash of thunder and lightning. Thus Barbara is patroness of powder magazines, fortifications, artillerymen, firefighters, and all who are exposed to sudden and violent death.

ST. BARTHOLOMEW (*It*. Bartolommeo, *Fr*. Barthélemy, *Sp*. Bartolomé, *Ger*. Bartholomäus), one of the lesser known of the twelve Apostles. He is easily distinguished in art by the large knife which he holds, in reference to the legend of his horrible martyrdom in Armenia where he was flayed alive. In his other hand, he often holds a book, the Gospel of St. Matthew, which he is said to have carried with him while preaching the gospel as far as India. In Michael Pacher's "Altarpiece of the Four Latin Fathers" [Munich, *464*] a statuette of Bartholomew with knife and book is painted to the right of *St. Gregory*. Sometimes, as in Michelangelo's *Last Judgment* [*540*], Bartholomew is shown holding the very skin that was stripped from his body.

ST. CATHERINE OF ALEXANDRIA (*It.* Catarina, *Sp.* Catalina, *Ger.* Katharina), third century, a virgin princess of Egypt, who, among the female saints, ranks in popularity just after *Mary Magdalen*, with whom she is often represented [*518*]. A Christian counterpart of the goddess Athena, she is noted for her beauty, wisdom and eloquence. She is patroness of learning, of scholars, schools and colleges, and, therefore, is often depicted with *St. Jerome* or another of the learned Doctors of the Church. Her special attribute is the spiked wheel, part of the machine devised by the Emperor Maximin to tear apart her body as punishment for having converted the fifty philosophers whom he had futilely employed to reason against her overwhelming arguments for the Faith. Catherine's wheel is often shown broken as a sign of her deliverance from Maximin's sentence when an angel broke the machine with such violence that fragments killed thousands of pagan onlookers. Catherine is also often shown holding the sword with which she was finally beheaded after rejecting the emperor's offer of marriage. So great was her beauty that even after she had converted the fifty philosophers, the emperor's wife, his most trusted counselor, and his soldiers, all of whom he had executed, Maximin offered to make her empress of the world. Catherine, however, had already chosen Christ as her spouse; her "Mystic Marriage," in which the Christ Child places a ring on her finger, is often represented as a separate subject.

ST. CHRISTOPHER (*It.* Cristoforo, *Fr.* Christophe, *Sp.* Cristóbal, *Ger.* Christophorus), third century?, a giant from the land of Canaan, who sought to put his great strength at the service of the most powerful monarch in the world. First he served a rich and powerful king, who, nonetheless, trembled before the name of Satan. Seeing this, Christopher then served Satan himself until one day the Prince of Evil admitted his fear of Christ when he avoided a roadside cross. Christopher then set out to find Christ. He asked the advice of a holy hermit who, when Christopher refused to fast or pray, suggested that he might serve Christ by carrying travellers across a deep and swollen river; then, the hermit said, Christ might appear to him. Christopher did this and one night he was awakened by the voice of a small boy who asked to be carried across the river. Christopher placed the child on his shoulders, but, as he waded across the river, a great storm blew up, the child became heavier and heavier, and he was barely able to reach the opposite bank without going under. When Christopher finally set the child safely down he asked, "Who art thou, child, that hath placed me in such extreme peril? Had I carried the whole world on my shoulders, the burden had not been heavier!" And the child answered, "Wonder not, Christopher, for thou hast not only borne the world, but Him who made the world, upon thy shoulders."

Christopher, whose name means "Christ-bearer," is often represented [*466*] in midstream, leaning on the uprooted palm tree which he used as a staff; he struggles beneath the load of the Christ Child who raises one hand in blessing and carries the orb of the world in the other. In the Ghent Altarpiece [*445*], Christopher, since he is the patron saint of travellers, leads the Holy Pilgrims at the extreme right. The prominent date palm (growing in the middle ground behind the giant), while it is a symbol of everlasting life, may also have been intended as an allusion to Christopher's palm-tree staff, which miraculously bore fruit when Christ told him to plant it in the earth as proof of his identity.

ST. DOROTHY (*It.* Dorotea, *Fr.* Dorothée, *Sp.* Dorotea, *Ger.* Dorothea), d. c. 300, a Christian virgin of the city of Caesarea in Cappadocia, was renowned for her beauty and piety. Brought before the governor of the city, a terrible persecutor of the Christians, she was commanded to worship the pagan gods or die. She explained that she would gladly accept death so that she might join Christ, her betrothed, in the gardens of Paradise where fruits and roses are eternally fresh. While Dorothy was being led away to be decapitated, a lawyer named Theophilus called out and mockingly asked her to send him some of the fruits and flowers, of which she had spoken, when she got to heaven. Upon her arrival at the place of execution, a beautiful boy suddenly appeared at her side carrying a basket of fresh fruit and flowers even though it was still winter. Dorothy, just before she died, asked the boy to take the basket to Theophilus and tell him that she had sent it. When Theophilus ate of the heavenly fruit, he was converted and willingly suffered martyrdom himself. The basket of fruit and flowers, usually apples and roses, is Dorothy's special attribute which she carries together with the palm or crown of martyrdom. When she is not accompanied by other saints, the basket is often carried by the child who may be given a cruciform nimbus to identify him as the Christ Child [*465*].

ST. FRANCIS OF ASSISI (*It.* Francesco, *Fr.* François, *Sp.* Francisco, *Ger.* Franziskus *or* Franz), 1181/2–1226, the son of a well-to-do merchant, abandoned a carefree life spent in the pursuit of pleasure for one of simplicity and poverty dedicated to the service of God. He was joined by others in his attempt to revive the humble life of the disciples of Christ and eventually Pope Innocent III granted St. Francis and his followers recognition as an order of mendicant friars and approved the simple rules of the order which required chastity, poverty, and obedience, but, above all, poverty. Thousands joined the new order and were sympathetically received by the people who were impressed by their simple way of life and their popular sermons which emphasized the charity and humanity of Christ. St. Francis is represented in the plain habit of his order, a long robe, originally gray but now brown, tied with a length of common rope [colorplate 31]. Sometimes he bears the "stigmata" [*552*], the wounds of the crucified Christ which were miraculously imprinted on his hands, feet and side while he was fasting alone on Mount Alverna [colorplate 35].

ST. GEORGE (*It.* Giorgio, *Fr.* Georges, *Sp.* Jorge, *Ger.* Georg), d. c. 300, a Christian tribune from Cappadocia in Asia Minor, who, during the persecutions ordered by the Emperor Diocletian, renounced his command and was finally beheaded after attempts to kill him with poisoned wine, a sword-studded wheel, and boiling lead had failed through divine intervention.

St. George is the patron saint of England, Portugal, and Germany and the patron saint of all soldiers and armorers. He is represented as a handsome young knight [*290*] and is usually distinguished from other knights by a red cross on his shield or banner, as in the Ghent Altarpiece [*445*] or in the statue of St. George which Donatello carved for the armorers' and swordsmiths' guild of Florence [*474*]. The relief beneath Donatello's statue [*475*] and the relief on the base of the lectern used by the singing angels in the Ghent Altarpiece [*445*] are representations of St. George killing the dragon, a symbol of the triumph of good over evil or, more specifically, of the triumph of Christianity over the Devil. The dragon, according to legend, threatened the town of Silene in Libya. To placate the monster, whose breath was poisoning the air, the citizens were reduced to giving it their sons and daughters to feed upon. One day, the lot fell to the king's daughter. As she was approaching the dragon's lair, St. George rode up and, making the sign of the cross, wounded the monster with his lance. St. George told the princess to put her girdle about the dragon's neck and she and St. George led it back to the city like a dog on a leash. St. George finally dispatched the beast after the people of Silene agreed to be baptized.

ST. GREGORY THE GREAT (*It.* Gregorio, *Fr.* Grégoire, *Sp.* Gregorio, *Ger.* Gregor), c. 540–604, one of the Four Latin Fathers of the Church, was born at Rome where he was appointed prefect of the city; after a period of monastic withdrawal, he served as deacon and as nuncio to Constantinople, and finally became pope, as Gregory I, in 590. Gregory was both a great scholar, in whose works the basic dogma of the church is fully developed, and a superb administrator, who during his reign saved Rome from the Lombards, began the conversion of Britain, and established rules for the clergy (including mandatory celibacy) and rules for the performance of ritual and liturgical chant. Gregory is represented in the rich vestments of a pope and crowned with the papal tiara; he usually holds a book in reference to his many theological works and the inspiring *dove* of the Holy Ghost sometimes hovers close to his ear. Some paintings show Gregory raising the Emperor Trajan from the flames of Hell [*464*] in accordance with the story that one day he was so moved while meditating on the piety of Trajan, who had given his own son as a slave to the mother of a man whom the son had accidentally killed, that he prayed for the release of the dead emperor's soul from the torments of Hell.

ST. HELENA, c. 250–c. 330, the mother of the Emperor Constantine the Great, became a Christian and while on a pilgrimage to Jerusalem discovered the True Cross, her customary attribute [*498*, colorplate *32*].

ST. JAMES THE GREAT (*It.* Giacomo, *Fr.* Jacques, *Sp.* Santiago, *Ger.* Jakobus), one of the twelve Apostles, was the brother of *St. John the Evangelist*. In the gospel accounts, James, John, and *St. Peter* are often called apart from the other disciples by Jesus; they were chosen to witness the *Transfiguration* and to accompany Christ during the *Agony in the Garden*. After the *Ascension*, James spread the gospel throughout the world, going as far as Spain where he is revered as the national saint. Returning to Judea, he was beheaded by order of Herod Agrippa and thus received the distinction of being the first of the Apostles to be martyred. The incidents of his martyrdom were painted by Mantegna on the walls of the Ovetari Chapel in the Erimitani Church in Padua [*516*]. James' body was sent to Spain where, after being lost during the Moslem incursions, it was enshrined at Compostela which became the most important pilgrimage center in Western Europe. St. James is often represented as a pilgrim to his own shrine, as in the group of Holy Pilgrims in the Ghent Altarpiece where he appears behind the giant *St. Christopher* [*445*]. He is usually shown leaning on a pilgrim's staff and wearing the pilgrim's great cloak, large wallet, and flap-brimmed hat with scallop shell.

ST. JEROME (*It.* Geronimo *or* Girolamo, *Fr.* Jérome, *Sp.* Jerónimo, *Ger.* Hieronymus), c. 340–420, one of the Four Latin Fathers of the Church, was born in Dalmatia and studied at Rome where he became a priest and secretary to the pope, but, being of an irascible temperament, he retired to the Holy Land, where he had lived as a hermit, and, settling at Bethlehem, spent the rest of his long life translating and interpreting the Bible. Jerome's Latin translation of the Bible (the Vulgate) became the standard Catholic text. He is usually represented as an old, bearded scholar holding the Vulgate in his hand [*518*] or working on his translation in his study, but he is also shown in the wilderness as a penitent ascetic. Sometimes he is accompanied by the lion he tamed by removing a thorn from its paw and quite frequently he is shown with a crimson cardinal's hat although the rank was not instituted until long after his death.

ST. JOHN THE BAPTIST (*It.* Giovanni Battista, *Fr.* Jean Baptiste, *Sp.* Juan Bautista, *Ger.* Johannes der Täufer), considered the last prophet of the Old Testament and the first saint of the New Testament, was the forerunner of Christ, who he hailed as the Messiah. Conceived six months before Christ, by Elizabeth, the wife of Zacharias, John lept for joy in his mother's womb when during the *Visitation* [*352*] the Virgin Mary, Elizabeth's cousin, announced that she had conceived the Son of God (Luke 1: 39–44). Even as an infant, John is shown reverently kneeling before the Christ Child [*523*]. John became an ascetic living in the wilderness of Judea, "his raiment of camel's hair, and a leathern girdel about his loins; and his meat was locusts and wild honey" (Matthew 3: 4). John is readily identified by his rude camel's skin tunic, which he wears under even the richest robes, as well as by his lean, ascetic figure and his long, unkempt hair and beard [colorplate 31]. People went to John in the wilderness to be baptized, as a sign of repentence, and he told them of the coming of the Messiah. Jesus himself came from Galilee to Jordan to be baptized by John [*358*]. Because John hailed Jesus as the "Lamb of God, which taketh away the sin of the world" (John 1: 29), the lamb is John's chief attribute [*447, 566, 579*]. John was eventually imprisoned by King Herod for speaking out against his marriage to his brother's wife, Herodias, and was finally beheaded at the request of Salome, the daughter of Herodias [*477*] (Matthew 14: 3–11; Mark 6: 17–28). John is of very high rank in the heavenly hierarchy and regularly appears with the Virgin Mary at the side of Christ as an intercessor pleading for mankind [colorplates 27, 45]. When Mary, John, and the enthroned Christ are treated as a separate subject, the group is called the *Deësis* [*290, 445*].

ST. JOHN THE EVANGELIST (*It.* Giovanni, *Fr.* Jean, *Sp.* Juan, *Ger.* Johannes) and his brother *St. James the Great* were fishermen of Galilee and among the first disciples of Christ. With *St. Peter* they formed an inner group among the disciples which received the special confidence of Jesus. John, the youngest of the disciples, is sometimes called the "Beloved Disciple" because he is identified with the one "whom Jesus loved" and "leaned on Jesus' bosom" at the *Last Supper* [499] (John 13: 23). During the *Crucifixion*, when Jesus saw Mary and John standing at the foot of the cross [*284, 405, 492*], he said to Mary, "Woman, behold thy son!" and he told John, "Behold thy mother!" (John 19: 26, 27). In the various Passion scenes, John is usually shown comforting Mary [colorplates 23, 27, 29, *579*] or mourning the loss of his master [*430, 460*, colorplate 42]. After the Crucifixion, John is said to have taken Mary into his own home and after her death [*399*, colorplate 24] and Assumption to have preached the gospel throughout Judea with St. Peter. He settled at Ephesus and during the persecutions of the Emperor Domitian, he was taken to Rome where he is said to have miraculously survived an attempt to kill him with a cup of poisoned wine, one of his special attributes [*447*], and an attempt to boil him in oil. John was banished as a sorcerer to the island of Patmos, where he wrote the last book of the New Testament, called the "Apocalypse" or the "Revelation of St. John the Divine" (i.e., the theologian). He is also credited with the three epistles and the Gospel which bear his name. According to *St. Jerome*, the eagle is John's special attribute as one of the Four Evangelists [colorplate 20], because he soared aloft to contemplate the divinity of Christ, which he emphasizes more than the other Evangelists. In any group of the Apostles, John is usually quickly singled out by his prominent position (often near Peter or Christ) and by the youthfulness of his features. In the West, John is usually depicted as beardless and with long curly hair of a light color, frequently blond [*428, 493, 520, 524, 585*], despite his supposed death at a very advanced age of one hundred years or more, after returning to Ephesus from his exile on Patmos.

ST. LAWRENCE (*It.* Lorenzo, *Fr.* Laurent, *Sp.* Lorenzo, *Ger.* Laurentius *or* Lorenz), d. 258, a native of Spain, went to Rome where he became archdeacon during the papacy of Sixtus II. When Sixtus was condemned to die for refusing to renounce the faith, Lawrence wished to be martyred with him, but the pope told him that he should first distribute the treasure of the Church among the poor to prevent it from being seized by the state. When Lawrence was called before the Emperor Valerian to deliver the treasure, he came with a great crowd of the impoverished and the infirm and told Valerian that he must search for the treasure of the Church in heaven where the poor had stored it up. For his impudence, Lawrence was imprisoned, tortured and finally martyred on a gridiron placed over burning coals. While he was being roasted, Lawrence, who had joyously sought his martyrdom, called out merrily to Valerian: "I am well cooked on one side. Turn the other and eat!" Lawrence, like *St. Stephen* with whom he is often represented, is handsome, youthful, and mild; both wear the dalmatic (a long-sleeved outer tunic) proper to deacons. Lawrence's special attribute is the gridiron upon which he was martyred [*540*]. On the base of his statue on the south transept portal at Chartres [*398*] is a relief of Valerian being choked by a devil.

ST. LUCY (*It.* Lucia, *Fr.* Luce *or* Lucie, *Sp.* Lucia, *Ger.* Luzia), d. c. 300, a young virgin of a noble family of Syracuse whose fiancé had denounced her as a Christian when she gave away all her possessions to the poor. Lucy was martyred by a dagger thrust in the neck, but her usual attribute is a pair of eyes lying on a dish held in her hand [colorplate 31]. The eyes were probably first introduced as an indication of her name, which means "light," but according to a legend which seems to have been invented in explanation of the attribute, Lucy cut out her eyes and gave them to a suitor who had pursued her out of admiration for their dazzling beauty.

ST. LUKE THE EVANGELIST (*It.* Luca, *Fr.* Luc, *Sp.* Lucas, *Ger.* Lukas), a physician of Antioch, became a disciple of *St. Paul* and accompanied him to Rome. After Paul's martyrdom, according to one tradition, he went as a missionary to Greece where he was crucified, but according to the Greek tradition he died a natural death. He is regarded as the author of two books of the Bible, the Gospel which bears his name and the Acts of the Apostles. Luke is also the patron saint of painters since he is said to have won converts by exhibiting his own paintings of Christ and the Virgin. His special attribute is the winged ox [colorplate 19], which frequently appears in conjunction with the symbols of the other three Evangelists [*318, 396,* colorplate 13]. Since the ox was a sacrificial animal in antiquity, it is interpreted as referring to the emphasis Luke places on the priesthood of Christ.

ST. MARGARET (*It.* Margherita, *Fr.* Marguérite, *Sp.* Margarita, *Ger.* Margarete), d. c. 300, virgin martyr of Antioch and patron saint of women in childbirth. The dragon upon which Margaret usually stands and the cross which she holds [*452*] refer to an episode during her torture and imprisonment for refusing to renounce Christ and become the wife of Olybrius, governor of Antioch. Satan visited her dungeon in the form of a terrible dragon and, according to one version, swallowed her alive, but she made the sign of the cross and the monster's belly burst. Shortly before Olybrius had her beheaded, Margaret prayed that all pregnant women who called upon her name might be granted the safe delivery of a healthy baby.

ST. MARK THE EVANGELIST (*It.* Marco, *Fr.* Marc, *Sp.* Marcos, *Ger.* Markus), like his friend and fellow Evangelist *St. Luke,* was not one of the twelve Apostles, although he accompanied *St. Paul* and *St. Peter* on some of their missionary journeys. While Luke's gospel is sometimes called "St. Paul's Gospel" because Luke was Paul's disciple, Mark's is thought to be composed of the personal reminiscences of St. Peter, who converted Mark and called him his son (I Peter 5: 13). Mark is said to have become the first bishop of Alexandria where he was martyred by being dragged through the streets with a rope around his neck. In the ninth century, his body was stolen from his tomb at Alexandria by Venetians and buried on the site of the great church of San Marco [*280, 281*]. Mark's special attribute is the winged lion, which, according to one interpretation, is said to stand for the emphasis placed on Christ's royal dignity in his Gospel [*326, 361*]. In Dürer's painting, "The Four Apostles" [Munich, *585*], Mark, who was probably intended by Dürer to represent the choleric temperament, seems to have absorbed some of the fearful physical characteristics of his attribute [colorplate 17].

ST. MARY MAGDALEN (*It.* Maria Maddalena, *Fr.* La Madeleine, *Sp.* Maria Magdalena, *Ger.* Maria Magdalena), who is mentioned in the Gospels as a woman from whom Christ cast out seven devils (Luke 8: 2) and later witnessed his Passion and *Resurrection,* has been identified in the West, since the time of *St. Gregory the Great,* with the penitent sinner who anointed Christ's feet (Luke 7: 37, 38) and with Mary, the sister of Martha and Lazarus, who also anointed his feet (John 12: 3). Mary frequently appears in depictions of the *Bearing of the Cross* [colorplate 23], the *Crucifixion* [colorplate 27, *579*], the *Descent from the Cross* [colorplate 29], the *Lamentation* [*430, 437, 460*], and the *Entombment.* She is usually richly dressed, in allusion to her sinful life of luxury before her repentence; her hair is usually unbound and very long since she used it to wipe Christ's feet; her special attribute is the pyxis, or ointment jar, by which she is readily identified when she appears alone or as a patron saint [*452*]. In paintings of the *Descent from the Cross,* the *Lamentation,* and the *Entombment* she mourns near those very feet which she anointed while Christ lived. Mary was the first to see the risen Christ (John 20: 11–17), a subject which is sometimes represented separately and called the "Noli me Tangere" (Touch me not). It is said that, many years after the *Ascension* of Christ, Mary, together with Martha and Lazarus and other Christians, was seized by infidels and set adrift in a rudderless ship which was carried to Marseilles. After persuading the people of the city to give up their idols and be baptized, Mary retreated into the wilderness where, sustained by celestial food, she did penance for thirty years until she was borne aloft by angels. The penitent Magdalen is usually represented as a beautiful young woman, but Donatello carved her as a toothless old recluse, her wasted body covered with the snarled and tangled tresses which were once her sinful pride [*483*].

ST. MATTHEW THE EVANGELIST (*It.* Matteo, *Fr.* Matthieu, *Sp.* Mateo, *Ger.* Matthäus), one of the twelve Apostles, was a tax-collector (publican) at Capernaum where Christ approached him in the custom house and said: "Follow me" [colorplate 49, *631*] (Matthew 9: 9). Matthew, who was also called Levi, followed Christ and, after preparing a great feast for him [*565*] (Luke 5: 29, 30), joined the small band of disciples. After the *Ascension,* he preached "to the Hebrews" and, before traveling to Egypt and Ethiopia, is said to have written his gospel for them. According to the "Golden Legend," Matthew was stabbed in the back while praying at the altar of his Ethiopian church. Thus, he is sometimes represented with a sword, but his special attribute is the winged man [*564*], or angel, which is thought to be appropriate because Matthew begins his Gospel with the human ancestry of Christ and emphasizes his humanity. Like the other Evangelists, he is often shown writing his Gospel [*324*] and, when the symbols of the Four Evangelists are grouped together, Matthew may be represented by the winged man alone [colorplate 13, *318, 396*].

ST. MICHAEL (*It.* Michele, *Fr.* Michel, *Sp.* Miguel), the greatest of the archangels, whose name means "like unto God," is captain of the heavenly hosts, whom he led against Satan's rebellious angels during the great war in heaven (Revelation 12: 7–9). In the Book of Daniel (12: 1), he is described as "the great prince which standeth for the children of thy people." From being lord and protector of the Chosen People, he became patron saint of the Church Militant. Michael is also lord of the souls of the dead and therefore plays a prominent part in depictions of the *Last Judgment* [colorplate 27], in which he appears in full armor, frequently holding the scales of justice. In Signorelli's fresco of "The Damned Cast into Hell" [*521*], Michael appears as commander of the other archangels venerated by the Church: Gabriel and Raphael. Michael is always depicted winged, eternally youthful and as beautiful as the artist can make him [*266*, colorplate 13, left].

ST. PAUL (*It.* Paolo, *Sp.* Pablo, *Ger.* Paulus) was born at Tarsus of Jewish parents who named him Saul. He undertook rabbinical studies at Jerusalem and became a fanatical persecutor of the Christians. He was an approving witness to the stoning of *St. Stephen* (Acts 7: 58) and was on his way to Damascus to arrest any Christians he might find there when he was blinded by a light from heaven and heard the voice of Christ (Acts 9). This experience resulted in his conversion and he devoted the rest of his life to spreading the gospel of Christ as zealously as he had at first attacked it. St. Paul and *St. Peter* are frequently represented together or on either side of Christ [*264*, colorplate 45] since the two are considered to be the founders of the Church: Peter as Apostle to the Jews and Paul as Apostle to the Gentiles. Paul's customary attributes are the sword, with which he was martyred in Rome under Nero, and the book of his epistles to the faithful [*585*]. Among the Apostles, Peter, Paul and the youthful *St. John* are the most distinctly characterized. Paul has a high forehead, his hair is brown, and his beard is full; he has a long prominent nose and usually a very determined visage [*399*, colorplate 24].

ST. PETER (*It.* Pietro *or* Piero, *Fr.* Pierre, *Sp.* Pedro, *Ger.* Petrus), a fisherman of Galilee, was one of the first disciples of Christ. His name was Simon, but Jesus called him Cephas (Peter), which means "rock." In the Gospels, Peter frequently acts as the spokesman of the twelve disciples and was chosen by Christ as the leader of his Church: "thou art Peter, and upon this rock I will build my church" (Matthew 16: 18). The large key or keys, which are Peter's special attribute [*354, 520, 540,* colorplate 45, *552, 585*], signify the power to loose and bind which was granted to him by Christ: "whatsoever thou shalt bind on earth shall be bound in heaven: and whatsoever thou shalt loose on earth shall be loosed in heaven" (Matthew 16: 19). Peter was impetuous. He recognized Jesus as "the Christ, the Son of the living God" (Matthew 16: 16) and fervently swore that he was ready to follow him to prison and to death (Luke 22: 33). When the soldiers came to arrest Jesus, Peter struck out with a sword and cut off the ear of Malchus, a servant of the high priest [*406*] (John 18: 10], but, soon after, he thrice denied that he even knew Jesus (Mark 14: 66–72). After the *Ascension*, Peter spread the gospel throughout Asia Minor and then is said to have gone to

Rome where he was martyred on the cross. At his own request the cross was inverted and he was nailed to it upside down since he felt unworthy of being crucified in the same way as his master. Bramante's "Tempietto" [*529*] is thought to mark the place where he was martyred; his presumed burial place, beneath the high altar of the basilica of St. Peter's [*608*], is marked by Bernini's great bronze canopy (baldacchino). Bernini also encased the wooden chair, which is thought to be Peter's cathedra (episcopal throne), in a magnificent display of bronze sculpture at the far end of the basilica [*612*]. Peter is always clearly distinguishable when he appears among the Apostles or other saints. He is usually given a prominent place among them and is shown as a stolid, robust old man with plain but vigorous features; his face is rather square and is framed by a short, curly beard [colorplates 19, 24, *493*]; he may be balding [*518*, colorplate 45, *552*] and sometimes he is shown with a circular bald spot at the top of his head like a monk's tonsure [colorplate 22, *428*].

ST. SEBASTIAN (*It.* Sebastiano, *Fr.* Sébastien, *Ger.* Sebastian), d. 288?, an officer in the imperial guard and a favorite of the Emperor Diocletian, who nonetheless ordered him executed by archers for refusing to deny Christ. Although left for dead, Sebastian was nursed back to health by the widow of a martyred friend and again testified to his faith before Diocletian, who had him clubbed to death. Sebastian is represented as a handsome, almost nude, young man, bound to a tree or column, his body pierced with arrows. It is probably the ancient association of these arrows with Apollo, the archer whose darts brought pestilence and sudden death, that accounts for both the beauty of Sebastian and his veneration as a plague saint. The ruined triumphal arch to which Sebastian is tied in Mantegna's depiction of his martyrdom [Vienna, colorplate 34] is probably intended as an allusion to the decay of the pagan world, a theme familiar from representations of the *Nativity*.

ST. STEPHEN (*It.* Stefano, *Fr.* Étienne, *Sp.* Esteban, *Ger.* Stephanus *or* Stefan), d. 33, the first deacon and the first martyr; his story is told in the sixth and seventh chapters of the Acts of the Apostles. Accused of blasphemy, Stephen was brought before the council of the Jews in Jerusalem to whom he delivered a fiery sermon accusing them of stubbornness and blindness before the Holy Ghost. This so infuriated them that they "ran upon him with one accord, and cast him out of the city, and stoned him." Saul (later *St. Paul*) was among those who consented to his death. Stephen is represented as a young man dressed in the wide-sleeved dalmatic of a deacon. Despite the rather choleric temperament displayed in his denunciation of the Jews, his face is usually gentle, since "all that sat in the council . . . saw his face as it had been the face of an angel." In El Greco's "Burial of Count Orgaz" [Santo Tomé, Toledo, colorplate 45], Stephen assists *St. Augustine* in lowering the body into the grave; his martyrdom is depicted on his vestment. Stephen's particular attribute is the stone, or stones, of his martyrdom which sometimes lie on the Scriptures he frequently holds, as in the panel with the portrait of Étienne Chevalier [Berlin, 458] from a diptych by Jean Fouquet. Because Stephen was reburied with *St. Lawrence*, the two saints are often represented together, as on the south porch at Chartres [*398*] where a small figure of Saul looks up from the base of Stephen's statue. Stephen and Lawrence are both deacons, both martyrs, both young and of a mild disposition.

ST. THEODORE (*It.* Teodoro, *Sp.* Teodoro, *Ger.* Theodor), the name of two warrior saints of the late third century, St. Theodore Tyro of Amasea and St. Theodore Stratelates of Heraclea. The two may originally have been one and the same person whose separate identities may be accounted for by the development of different legends in separate localities. The two Theodores appear on the left-hand wing of the Harbaville Triptych [Louvre, *290*]. The handsome young knight on the left portal of the south porch at Chartres [*398*] should probably be identified as St. Theodore Tyro, since he is said to have set fire to a temple of Cybele and is shown in the act on one of the windows at Chartres; for this he was burned alive. On the base of the statue, Theodore is shown kneeling before an idol which, according to one legend, he later secretly broke up, distributing the precious pieces to the poor.

ST. THERESA OF AVILA (*It.* Teresa, *Fr.* Thérèse, *Sp.* Teresa, *Ger.* Theresia), 1515–1582, Spanish mystic, founder of the Discalced (Barefoot) Carmelite Order. Many of her visions are represented in the churches of the Order; the most famous is Bernini's group, usually known as "The Ecstasy of St. Theresa" [*610, 611*], in the Cornaro Chapel at the Carmelite Church of Sta. Maria della Vittoria, Rome. Bernini's representation corresponds exactly with Theresa's description of her "transverberation" (the piercing of her heart by the arrow of Divine Love), the vision mentioned in her Bull of canonization.

ST. THOMAS (*It.* Tommaso, *Sp.* Tomé), one of the twelve disciples of Christ, called "Doubting Thomas" because of his refusal to believe in the *Resurrection* until Christ appeared to him and he touched his wounds. Thomas is traditionally the Apostle to India, where he was martyred. He bears a lance, the instrument of his martyrdom, on the left wing of the Portinari Altarpiece [Uffizi, *452*]. More frequently, he holds a carpenter's square, as in El Greco's "Burial of Count Orgaz" [Santo Tomé, Toledo, colorplate 45]. The square alludes to a moralizing legend in which Thomas is directed by Gondoforus, King of the Indies, to build a magnificent palace. While the king is away, Thomas gives the gold for the palace to the sick and the poor, thereby assuring the king a palace in heaven rather than on earth. The legend has assured Thomas his position as patron saint of architects and builders.

CHAPTER FIVE

CHRISTIAN SIGNS AND SYMBOLS

APPLE. Although the fruit of the Tree of the Knowledge of Good and Evil in the Garden of Eden is not specified in the Bible (Genesis: Chapter 3), it was commonly thought to be an apple tree, perhaps because the Latin word for "apple" and for "sin" (*malum*) are the same. When Adam and Eve are shown with an apple [*583*] or some other fruit [*446*], it is a symbol of their sinfulness in disobeying the injunction of God not to eat the fruit of the Tree of Knowledge. When the apple is held by Mary or the infant Jesus, or when it simply appears near them [*468*], it alludes to their rôles as the Second Eve and the Second Adam who took away the sin of the first man and woman and restored to mankind the promise of eternal life.

BIRD. Birds of many species appear in Christian decoration, from the earliest times, as emblems of the soul [*259, 318, 518*]. In narrative representations, however, the soul is depicted as a little doll-like figure [*285*, upper right, *399*, colorplates 24, 45]. Particular species of birds have special meanings: the peacock is a symbol of immortality because it was thought that its flesh does not decay; the goldfinch, since it eats thorny plants, refers to Christ's *crown* of thorns and, therefore, to his Passion in general; the *eagle* is the attribute of St. John; the *dove* is the emblem of the Holy Ghost; and the *pelican* is an emblem of Christ's sacrifice.

CHALICE. A chalice, the metal drinking goblet used to hold the consecrated wine during the performance of the Eucharist (the sacrament of Holy Communion), refers to the *Last Supper* and to Christ's sacrifice on the Cross. At the Last Supper, when Jesus gave the cup of wine to his disciples, he said: "this is my blood of the new testament, which is shed for many for the remission of sins" (Matthew 26: 28). The identification of the Eucharistic wine with the sacrificial blood of the crucified Christ is made most directly in images of the *Lamb* of God in which the blood issuing from the breast of the Lamb flows directly into a large chalice [*445*, 579]. The cup of suffering,

117

mentioned by Christ during the *Agony in the Garden,* is usually represented as a Eucharistic chalice and sometimes appears among the *Instruments of the Passion.* The cup held by Melchizedek when he gives Abraham bread and wine [*401*] is also usually given the shape of a Eucharistic chalice since Melchizedek, the priest-king, was seen as an Old Testament type of Christ and his offering of wine was seen as a prefiguration of the *Last Supper.* The *serpent* or serpents in the chalice which *St. John the Evangelist* carries as an attribute [*447*], allude to various legends according to which he was given a cup of poisoned wine to drink.

CITY. In medieval church decoration and manuscript illumination, the City of God, the Heavenly Jerusalem described in the Revelation of St. John (Chapter 21), is usually represented in schematized form with crenellated walls and towers [chandelier in *319*; colorplate 19]. In Early Christian art, however, the image of the resplendent city is sometimes based on the type of ancient Roman stage setting elaborated in Pompeian wall decoration [cf. *245* and *259*]. On the Ghent Altarpiece [*445*], it is marked by a multitude of towers and turrets, rising above the horizon in the panels depicting the Adoration of the Lamb. The clusters of such towers, which were originally planned for many Romanesque and Gothic churches [*329, 345, 346*], were quite likely intended to convey the impression of the Heavenly City on earth described by St. John: "the city of my God, which is new Jerusalem, which cometh down out of heaven . . ." (Revelation 3: 12).

COLUMBINE. The columbine, which is called "ancolie" in French, was used in fifteenth- and sixteenth-century paintings as a symbol of melancholy and sorrow because of its name and its dark violet color. In paintings of the Virgin Mary it refers to her sorrow for her crucified son. When seven flowers are represented [*452*], they may refer to the Seven Sorrows of the Virgin: (1) the Prophecy of Simeon during the *Presentation in the Temple.* (2) the *Flight into Egypt.* (3) Jesus lost by his mother in Jerusalem. (4) the *Bearing of the Cross.* (5) the *Crucifixion.* (6) the *Descent from the Cross.* (7) the *Entombment.* However, the columbine (fr. L. columbinus, dovelike) may also be used as an emblem of the Holy Ghost because the flower resembles the shape of a *dove.* In this case, when there are seven flowers or seven petals on a flower, they refer to the Seven Gifts of the Holy Spirit: Wisdom, Understanding, Counsel, Strength, Knowledge, Piety, and Fear of the Lord (Isaiah 11: 2).

COLUMN. A single prominent column in a painting of the infancy of Christ [*452*] may be intended as an allusion to the column to which Christ was bound during his *Flagellation.* Thus, by foreshadowing the Passion of Christ through which mankind was saved, the column indicates the reason for the Incarnation. *See* INSTRUMENTS OF THE PASSION.

CROSIER (croh'zher), the ornate staff, resembling a shepherd's crook, which is carried by bishops [colorplate 31, *463*], symbolizes their rôle as shepherds of the "flock of Christ."

CROSS. The cross is the most common emblem of Christ and his Church. Since it is the chief instrument of his Passion, the cross is a sign of the sacrifice through which mankind won redemption and salvation. When the cross surmounts a *globe* [*466*], it is a sign of the triumph of Christ and Christianity over the world; when it is placed atop an obelisk [*607*], it specifically refers to triumph over the pagan world. The cross may even appear, somewhat anachronistically, in paintings of the infant Christ as an allusion to his future sacrifice [garden gate in colorplate 46, *552*] and as an indication of the reason for his Incarnation. Some fifty forms of the cross have commonly been used in Christian art and church decoration; some of the most frequently encountered forms and the names by which they are usually known are indicated below.

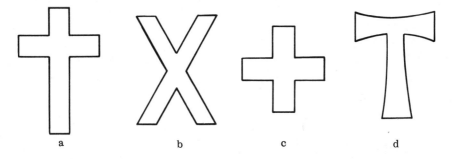

Fig. 56. Types of crosses: (a) Latin, (b) St. Andrew's, (c) Greek, (d) Tau.

CROWN. A crown is a symbol of victory or of royalty. It is the chief attribute of emperors, kings and queens [*271*, colorplate 14, *357*, *397*] and is worn by God the Father, Christ, and the Virgin Mary as a sign of their sovereignty over the kingdom of heaven [*402*, colorplate 24, *414*, *463*]. When the three persons of the *Trinity* are represented by a single figure [*445*], he may wear the papal tiara, a triple crown surmounted by a cross [*464*]. The crown of thorns which Christ wears in depictions of his Passion [*408*, colorplate 29, *555*] was placed on his head in mockery (Matthew 27: 29) but it is a sign of his suffering and of his triumph over death. Martyrs are also sometimes shown wearing or carrying crowns as a sign of their victory over death [*465*].

DEAD TREE. According to a medieval tradition alluded to in many fifteenth- and sixteenth-century paintings, the Tree of the Knowledge of Good and Evil withered when Adam and Eve, disobeying God, ate of its fruit, but was restored to life through Christ's sacrifice on the Cross. Thus, a conspicuously dead tree in a painting of the "Fall of Man" [colorplate 38], the *Nativity* [*443*], the Passion [*430*], or the *Resurrection* [colorplate 46] may refer to the original sin of Adam and the redemption of mankind through Christ.

DOG. The dog, "man's best friend," is a common emblem of faithfulness in marriage [*449*] and religion [*584*].

DOVE. The third person of the Trinity, the Holy Ghost, is represented as a dove in accordance with the descriptions of its descent upon Jesus during his *Baptism* (Matthew 3: 16, Mark 1: 10, Luke 3: 22). The dove of the Holy Ghost regularly appears in representations of the *Trinity* [*492*], the *Baptism*

[*358*], and the *Annunciation* [*447*, colorplate 46]. [*Also see* colorplate 20, *445, 463, 464, 612, 621*].

DRAGON. The dragon is an emblem of evil and is often identified with Satan, who may assume the form of a dragon [*332*] rather than that of a *serpent* or demon of more or less human form. On the central panel of the Portinari Altarpiece [*452*], Satan appears as a dragon-like demon above the head of the ox. He is caught between the column and the wall, frustrated and angry because he has been trapped by the Incarnation. The mouth of Hell, the realm of Satan, was frequently represented as a great dragon's head devouring the bodies of the damned [*581*]. Among the saints, *George* [*475*] and *Michael* fought the evil dragon and *Margaret* was swallowed by a dragon, but she split him open with a cross and as a sign of her triumph is often shown standing on his head, as on the right-hand panel of the Portinari Altarpiece [*452*].

EAGLE. The eagle is the attribute of *St. John the Evangelist* and, according to tradition, symbolizes the soaring spirit of John in his contemplation of the divine nature of Christ [colorplate 20]. John's eagle frequently appears with the symbols of the other Evangelists: the winged man of *St. Matthew*, the *lion* of *St. Mark*, and the *ox* of *St. Luke* [colorplate 13, *318, 396*].

FOUNTAIN. The "fountain of life" or the "fountain of living waters" is used as a symbol of salvation in various books of the Old Testament and in the Revelation of St. John (7: 17; 21: 6). An inscription based on Revelation 22: 1 appears on the basin of the prominent fountain on the interior of the Ghent Altarpiece [*445*] identifying it as the "fountain of life proceeding out of the throne of God and the Lamb." From a spout at the base of the fountain issues the "pure river of water of life, clear as crystal" which is described in the same passage. During the fifteenth and sixteenth century the identification of Christ with the "fountain of life" or the "well of living water" was so complete that the crucified Christ was shown as a fountain: blood spurts from his wounds into a basin and flows from there into a Eucharistic chalice. Claus Sluter's "Well of Moses" [*410*], when it was surmounted with a crucifix, presented a three-dimensional image of the mystic fountain. Mary is also associated with a fountain; sometimes, when she is depicted in the enclosed *garden*, the "fountain of gardens" or the "well of living waters" of the Song of Songs (4: 15) is shown nearby. The *wash basin* and water pitcher in Flemish paintings of the Virgin [colorplate 28, *444, 447*] may have been intended as an indoor equivalent of the fountain or well.

GARDEN. When the Virgin Mary is represented within or near a garden surrounded by a wall [*444, 468, 497*, colorplate 46] the garden refers to the "garden enclosed" (L., *hortus conclusus*) of the Song of Songs (4: 12). It is one of the many metaphors of chastity which were taken from the poem and given visual form in fifteenth- and sixteenth-century paintings of the Virgin.

GLASS. A transparent glass window or vase through which rays of *light* pass was sometimes used in fifteenth- and sixteenth-century paintings of the Virgin Mary as a disguised symbol of the Virgin Birth [colorplates 28, 46]. The symbol is derived from a medieval Nativity hymn in which an analogy is drawn between the miraculous birth and the phenomenon of light passing through glass without breaking it.

GLOBE. The globe or orb is a symbol of the world. When it is held in the left hand by Christ or by God the Father, it is a sign of their sovereignty [*402, 463, 466*]. When a *cross* surmounts the globe, it is a symbol of the triumph of Christ and of Christianity over the world [*266, 505, 546, 608*].

GRAPES are a symbol of the Eucharist, the sacrament of the Lord's Supper (Holy Communion). As *wheat* refers to the bread which Christ said was his body, grapes refer to the wine which he said was his blood: "And he took the cup, and gave thanks, and gave it to them, saying. Drink ye all of it; For this is my blood of the new testament, which is shed for many for the remission of sins" (Matthew 26: 28). When the Christ Child holds a bunch of grapes [*495*] it is a sign of his earthly mission and foreshadows his Passion.

HALO. The halo or nimbus is a conventional symbol of radiant *light* placed around the heads of saints as an indication of their holiness. Originally, however, it was a mark of distinction placed around the heads of gods and kings; in S. Vitale at Ravenna, for example, the mosaic images of the Emperor Justinian and the Empress Theodora are given imperial haloes even though they were living when the mosaics were made and certainly never became saints [*271*, colorplate 14]. The tradition also survives in representations of Buddha [*838, 840*]. Haloes are usually circular, but sometimes God the Father is given a triangular halo signifying the Trinity [*479*] and sometimes living persons, such as donors, are distinguished from the saints by square haloes. Only Christ is given a cruciform nimbus [colorplates 15, 19, 22, 24] because it refers directly to his sacrifice on the Cross.

HAND. A large hand or arm issuing from the heavens is a direct translation in visual terms of the "Hand" or "Arm of the Lord" frequently used in the Bible as a metaphor of the power and will of God [colorplate 20].

HOURGLASS. The movement of the grains of sand as they fall from the upper compartment of an hourglass to the lower is a sign of the unceasing passage of time and a symbol of the brevity of human life. As such, it is an appropriate attribute of the *skeleton* of Death [*584*].

INSTRUMENTS OF THE PASSION is the term usually applied to the implements used in the *Crucifixion* of Christ or associated with his suffering during the Passion. The chief instrument of the Passion is the *cross*, but many others, such as the *nails, lance, sponge, column, crown of thorns, chalice,* and *wash basin,* may be presented quite apart from any rendering of a specific moment of the Passion. They may appear, for example, in depictions of the *Last Judgment* [colorplate 27, *538*] where they are emblems of Christ's right to judge mankind, in representations of Christ as the Man of Sorrows or the *Lamb* of God [*445*], or even heraldically grouped as an emblem in a kind of picture writing summarizing the chief events of the Passion. Other common Instruments, besides those already mentioned and treated in separate entries, are the lantern, torch, rope, sword, club, staff, and the purse of Judas [all associated with the *Betrayal*], the cat-o'-nine-tails and scourges of the *Flagellation*, a crowing rooster alluding to the *Denial of Peter*, and the ladder, hammer, pincers, robe, and dice (John 19: 23, 24) associated with the *Crucifixion* itself.

IRIS. The iris, which was known in Latin as the "gladiolus," or "sword-lily," because of its sword-shaped leaves, appears in fifteenth- and sixteenth-century paintings of the Virgin and Child [*452*] as a disguised symbol foreshadowing the grief of Mary at the *Crucifixion* of Christ. The iris replaced the more obvious symbol of the sword which was formerly shown stuck in Mary's heart in allusion to old Simeon's prophecy to Mary during the *Presentation in the Temple:* "Yea, a sword shall pierce through thy own soul also" (Luke 2: 35).

KEYS. One or two large keys are the special attribute of *St. Peter* and distinguish him from other bearded, balding and white-haired old men [colorplate 45, *552*, *585*]. The keys allude to the passage in the Gospel of St. Matthew (16: 19) in which Christ, addressing Peter, says: "And I will give unto thee the keys of the kingdom of heaven." The *Delivery of the Keys to St. Peter* is represented in the fresco by Perugino on one of the side walls of the Sistine Chapel [*520*]. Since this act is interpreted as a token of the transmission of authority from Christ to Peter, who is considered the first pope, the keys are a prominent feature of the papal coat of arms [*608, 612*].

LAMB. The lamb, used as a sacrificial animal in antiquity, is most commonly used as a symbol of Christ's redeeming sacrifice on the Cross. In the New Testament, Christ is frequently referred to as the Lamb. *John the Baptist*, upon seeing Christ, says: "Behold the Lamb of God, which taketh away the sin of the world" (John 1: 29). And in the Revelation of *St. John the Evangelist*, which is the primary literary source for the "Adoration of the Lamb" in the Ghent Altarpiece [*445*], the Lamb is used throughout as a metaphor for Christ: "And I looked and, lo, a Lamb stood on the mount Sion, and with him an hundred forty and four thousand . . ." (14: 1). The Lamb of God (L. *Agnus Dei*) is usually represented with a wound in its side from which blood flows into a *chalice* [*445*]; one leg is frequently lifted to hold a cross [*579*] which often has a pennant of triumph flying from it to indicate Christ's triumph over death. The lamb is the special attribute of St. John the Baptist [*566, 447*] and *St. Agnes*. In Early Christian art, the lamb is not only used as a symbol of Christ, but is also used to represent the Apostles and all Christians in general. The twelve lambs at the base of the semi-dome of the apse of S. Apollinare in Classe [colorplate 13] represent the twelve Apostles; the three lambs, further up, represent the three disciples who accompanied Christ to the Mount of the *Transfiguration;* and the lambs, along the arch, represent the faithful issuing from the city gates of Jerusalem and Bethlehem, symbolizing the union of Jews and Gentiles through Christ. As the Good Shepherd [*252*] of the parables (Luke 15: 3–7, John 10: 1–18), Christ is shown with the lambs of his flock. On the sarcophagus of Junius Bassus [Vatican, 263], the subjects from both the Old Testament and the New Testament, which are carved on the spandrels (the Three Children in the Fiery Furnace, Moses Striking Water from the Rock, the Multiplication of the Loaves, and the *Baptism* of Christ), are enacted by lambs rather than by human figures.

LANCE, one of the *Instruments of the Passion* and the attribute of both St.

Longinus, the centurion who pierced the side of Christ [colorplate 27], and *St. Thomas* the Apostle [*452*]. The warrior saints, such as *St. George* [*445*] and *St. Theodore* [*290, 398*] also regularly carry lances as part of their military equipment.

LIGHT. Light is one of the most ancient signs of divinity and holiness. The imagery of light as goodness and wisdom and darkness as ignorance and evil is used throughout both the Old and the New Testaments, but it especially pervades the Gospel of St. John in which Christ himself says: "I am the Light of the World" (8: 12), a sentence which in Latin is "Ego sum lux mundi" and frequently occurs in church decoration [*508*]. The *halo* and *mandorla* are conventional symbols of radiant light and were the devices most frequently used to indicate the holiness of Christ and the saints in medieval art, but more illusionistic devices have been used from time to time, especially in depictions of the persons of the Trinity. In early Christian mosaics, for example, Christ sometimes appears against a glorious sunset sky of many hues [colorplate 13]. With the preference for more illusionistic modes of representation in the late Middle Ages and the Renaissance, amorphous glories or aureoles radiate from the body and, for a time, haloes were foreshortened in such a way that they appeared to be golden plates riveted to the heads of the saints [colorplate 22, *492, 493*] or hoops of gold hovering above them [colorplate 31], but these obviously artificial emblems were generally given up by the sixteenth century when the holy figures either appeared without any indication of supernatural illumination or were given amorphous glories and aureoles which, except for their emanation from human bodies, approximated the effect of normal sources of illumination [*454*, colorplate 46, *559*]. In Baroque sculpture and architecture, concealed sources of natural light were sometimes used in rather dark interiors to flood the holy figures and emblems with an apparently supernatural light and cause the gilt rays surrounding them to glisten [*610, 611, 615, 621*]. Occasionally, stained glass was also used [*612*], as in Gothic church windows [*367*, colorplate 21, *420, 421*], to transmute natural light into an apparently supernatural radiance emanating from within the holy image itself.

LILY. The lily is a symbol of purity and is therefore frequently used as an emblem of the Virgin Mary [*508*]. In representations of the *Annunciation*, lilies are often shown in a vase [*444*, colorplate 28] or held by the Archangel Gabriel [*447*] as a sign of Mary's chastity at the moment of the Incarnation. The species of lily most particularly identified with the Virgin is the *Lilium Candidum*, or Madonna Lily.

LION. The lion, usually winged, is the attribute of *St. Mark*, one of the Four Evangelists [*326*, colorplate 17, *361*]. According to one interpretation, the lion alludes to the emphasis Mark places on the majesty of Christ in his Gospel. According to another, it refers to his extensive treatment of the *Resurrection*, since an analogy was drawn between the three days that elapsed between Christ's death on the Cross and his Resurrection with the three days that were thought to pass between the birth of lion cubs (which were supposedly always stillborn) and their awakening to life when their sire roared or breathed upon them. The lion is frequently grouped with the symbols of the other Evangelists: the winged man of *St. Matthew*, the winged *ox* of *St. Luke*, and the *eagle* of *St. John* [colorplate 13, *318*, *396*]. The lion that accompanies *St. Jerome* is the one who faithfully followed the saint after he took compassion on the suffering beast and extracted a thorn from its paw.

MANDORLA (It., almond), a large oval surrounding the figure of God, Christ, the Virgin, and, on rare occasions, the saints as a symbol of divinity or holiness [*286*, *354*, colorplate 19, *396*].

MONOGRAMS OF CHRIST. Many monograms and abbreviations of the name of Christ occur from time to time in works of art. Some of the most common are explained below:

☧ The two Greek letters Chi (X) and Rho (P), the first two letters of the Greek word for Christ, were combined by the early Christians so that they formed a cross [*271*]. Sometimes the first and last letters of the Greek alphabet, Alpha (A) and Omega (W), are placed to either side of the cross in allusion to a passage in the Revelation of St. John (1:8): "I am Alpha and Omega, the beginning and the ending, saith the Lord . . ."

IHS or IHC. In the later Middle Ages, the IHS and IHC monograms became more popular than the Chi Rho symbol. They are derived from the first three letters of the Greek word for Jesus, which is spelled either "Ihsus" or "Ihcuc." Very often the horizontal line above the monogram, which indicates that it is an abbreviation, intersects the "h" to form a cross and sometimes a cross is placed above the crossbar of the "H" [*577*]. According to a more recent tradition, the IHS stands for the Latin phrase "Iesus Hominum Salvator" (Jesus, Saviour of Mankind).

IC XC. A very common abbreviation in Byzantine art [*279*, *286*, *290*, colorplate 15] is derived from the first and last letters of the Greek "Ihcuc" (Jesus) and "Xpictoc" (Christ). The horizontal line which usually appears over each pair of letters indicates that it is an abbreviation.

I. N. R. I. The letters frequently placed on a tablet or scroll attached to the cross of the crucified Christ [*579*] are an abbreviation of the Latin inscription "Iesus Nazarenus Rex Iudaeorum" which, according to the Gospel of St. John (19:19–22), Pilate placed on the cross:

And Pilate wrote a title, and put it on the cross. And the writing was, JESUS OF NAZARETH THE KING OF THE JEWS. This title then read many of the Jews: for the place where Jesus was crucified was nigh to the city: and it was written in Hebrew, and Greek, and Latin. Then said the chief priests of the Jews to Pilate, Write not, The King of the Jews; but that he said, I am King of the Jews. Pilate answered, What I have written I have written.

Sometimes the whole trilingual inscription is written out [*627*].

NAILS. Large nails or spikes, held by an angel or appearing in association with other *Instruments of the Passion*, signify the suffering of Christ while he was nailed to the cross [*461*, colorplate 27]. The hammer with which the nails were driven into his flesh and the pincers with which they were withdrawn are often shown as well.

OX. A winged ox is the attribute of *St. Luke,* one of the Four Evangelists [colorplate 19]. The ox, holding a book (the Gospel of St. Luke), frequently appears together with the winged man of *St. Matthew,* the winged *lion* of *St. Mark,* and the *eagle* of *St. John.* The ox, a sacrificial animal [colorplate 12], presumably alludes to Luke's emphasis on the priesthood of Christ. The twelve oxen at the base of the baptismal font by Renier of Huy, in the church of S. Barthélemy in Liège, are symbols of the twelve Apostles [*358*]. They were probably suggested by the description (II Chronicles 4: 4) of the great basin set up by Solomon for the ablutions of the priests in the Temple at Jerusalem.

PALM BRANCH, an ancient Roman symbol of Victory; in Christian art, it is the attribute of martyrs, symbolizing their triumph over death [*445, colorplate 31, 518*].

PALM TREE. The palm tree, because it is always green, was frequently used in Early Christian art as a symbol of the promise of immortality [colorplate 13, *445*].

PELICAN. The image of a pelican piercing her breast with her beak and feeding her young with her own blood is a symbol of Christ's self-sacrifice for the salvation of man. This image of loving sacrifice, sometimes called the "Pelican in her Piety," is derived from descriptions in medieval bestiaries (books on the habits of beasts). It is repeated many times in the brocade behind the figure of God on the Ghent Altarpiece [*445*].

ROSES. In representations of the Virgin, roses are an emblem of her charity [*444, 468,* colorplate 46]. The rose was formerly the flower of Venus, goddess of Love. Mary herself is called "the rose without thorns."

RUINS, usually Roman or Romanesque, are found in representations of the birth of Christ as signs of that decay of the pagan world which, from the Christian point of view, made the Incarnation necessary [colorplate 26, *443, 452*].

SCROLL. In later Christian art, scrolls, the older form of manuscript, are frequently used as attributes of the Old Testament prophets and the pagan sibyls who foretold the coming of Christ [*351, 426, 447,* colorplates 19, 43].

SERPENT. In representations of the "Fall of Man," Satan appears in the guise of a serpent [*583*]. In Michelangelo's representation of the subject on the Sistine Ceiling [colorplate 38], Satan assumes the body of a beautiful temptress with a long serpent's tail. The serpent is also an ancient symbol of death [*435, 584*]. *St. John the Evangelist* is sometimes shown holding a cup with a serpent in it [*447*] in allusion to various stories according to which he was given a cup of poisoned wine.

SHOES. When shoes or sandals are prominently displayed in a picture in which figures stand barefoot or in their stocking feet, it is a sign that they are standing on holy ground [*449, 452,* colorplate 35; cf. *41*].

SKELETON. A human skeleton, or a human *skull,* is a "memento mori," or reminder of death; it is a forceful sign of the ephemeral character of life on earth and a check to the pursuit of worldly vanities [*435*]. Skeletons, representing the deceased, were sometimes carved or painted on late medieval tombs together with such admonitory inscriptions as: "What you are, I once was; what I am, you will be" [*492*] or simply "memento mori" ("Remember that you must die"). When a skeleton is animated, it is a personification of Death [colorplate 27] and may bear such attributes as an *hourglass, serpents* [*584*], a scythe with which to cut men down, or a pitchfork with which to toss them into Hell [*581*].

SKULL. Any skull, but especially a human skull, or death's-head, is a reminder of death (memento mori) suggesting the vanity of man's transitory life on earth [lower right corner of colorplate 45, *584*]. The skull frequently appears as an attribute of penitent saints and hermits [colorplate 35]. When a skull appears near the base of the cross of the crucified Christ [*284*, colorplate 29] it marks the site of the *Crucifixion* as Golgotha (Calvary), "the place of the skull" (John 19: 17). According to a medieval tradition, this was the burial place of Adam, whose disobedience lost for mankind the gift of eternal life and made it necessary for Christ to suffer on the cross so that man might be absolved of his sins and regain the promise of immortality. Sometimes, the blood trickles from the wounds of Christ down over the skull at the foot of the cross [*284*] symbolizing the washing away of Adam's sin and the sin of all mankind through Christ's sacrifice (Revelation 1: 5).

SPONGE. A sponge attached to the top of a staff is one of the *Instruments of the Passion* [colorplate 27, *445*]. It refers to the incident described in the accounts of the *Crucifixion* just before Christ cried aloud and gave up the ghost: "And straightway one of them ran, and took a sponge, and filled it with vinegar, and put it on a reed, and gave him to drink" (Matthew 27: 48). This may have been done as an act of mercy to quench his thirst, but it is traditionally regarded as a final act of humiliation in the long series of abuses against the person of Christ during the Passion.

TOWER. The fortified tower which appears in the backgrounds of many fifteenth- and sixteenth-century pictures of the Virgin Mary [*468*] refers to the Tower of David mentioned in the Song of Songs (4: 4) and was intended as a symbol of Mary's chastity. Jan van Eyck, in the painting of the *Annunciation* on the exterior of the Ghent Altarpiece [*447*] seems to have placed the Virgin inside the tower, far above the rooftops seen from the window of her high chamber.

TREFOIL. The trefoil, since it is a single figure composed of three lobes, is often used as a symbol of the three persons of the Trinity [*432, 447*].

TRIANGLE. The triangle, which like the *trefoil* is a single figure formed of three parts, is sometimes used as a symbol of the Trinity [*432, 615*]. Occasionally, the image of God the Father is given a triangular halo [*479*] to indicate the presence of the other two persons of the Trinity.

VINE. Vines, especially grapevines, have been used since the time of the early Christians [*264, 318, 399, 461,* colorplate 35] to allude to Christ's description of himself as a vine: "I am the true vine, and my Father is the husbandman . . . I am the vine, ye are the branches: He that abideth in me, and I in him, the same bringeth forth much fruit: for without me ye can do nothing"

(John 15: 1–5). When there are bunches of *grapes* on the vine, they refer to the sacrament of the Eucharist and to Christ's Passion.

VIOLETS symbolize humility and are therefore one of the flowers used to indicate aspects of the character of the Virgin Mary. When violets appear in representations of the *Annunciation* [*444*] and the *Nativity*, they may also refer to the humility of the Son of God as revealed in his incarnation.

WASH BASIN. In Flemish paintings of the Virgin Mary a wash stand or a niche, with a wash basin, a water pitcher (ewer), and a towel, sometimes appears as an emblem of Mary's chastity [colorplate 28, *447*]. The ewer and basin, besides being common signs of cleanliness and purity, may also have been intended as disguised symbols serving as indoor counterparts of the "spring shut up" and the "fountain sealed" or the "fountain of gardens" and the "well of living waters" (Song of Songs 4: 12, 4: 15) which were interpreted as metaphors of the Virgin. Sometimes a ewer and basin appear among the *Instruments of the Passion* in reference to the washing of guilt from Pilate's hands [colorplate 44; Matthew 27: 24].

WHEAT. A sheaf of wheat is sometimes included in representations of *Nativity* and *Adoration* scenes [*452*] as an emblem of the Incarnation and as a fore-shadowing of the *Last Supper* and the *Crucifixion*. In the Gospel of St. John (12: 24), Jesus, foretelling his death, compares himself to a grain of wheat: "Except a corn of wheat fall into the ground and die, it abideth alone: but if it die, it bringeth forth much fruit." Jesus also says that he is "the living bread which came down from heaven: if any man eat of this bread, he shall live for ever: and the bread that I will give is my flesh, which I will give for the life of the world" (John 6: 51). And, at the Last Supper, when he gives the bread to the disciples to eat, he says: "This is my body which is given for you: this do in remembrance of me" (Luke 22: 19). The sheaf of wheat, then, is a Eucharistic symbol revealing Christ's mission as the savior of mankind. It also alludes to the place of his birth, Bethlehem, which means "House of Bread."

WHEEL OF FORTUNE. A wheel with human figures along its rim, rising or falling as it revolves, is an emblem of the instability of Fortune and the vanity of wordly pursuits: as some of the figures rise to power and riches, others must inevitably fall [*422*].

ZODIAC. The twelve signs of the zodiac, which were often carved around the portals of Romanesque and Gothic churches together with emblems of the Labors of the Months, suggest the omnipresence and omnipotence of God throughout time and space and lend universal significance to the other subjects represented near them [*354, 396, 403*].

MAPS

ART CENTERS OF WESTERN EUROPE

SCOTLAND

Lindisfarne

Kells
Dublin
IRELAND

Durham

ENGLAND

Gloucester Blenheim   Sutton Hoo
Oxford
Dorchester
Chiswick
Stonehenge Twickenham London
Salisbury Canterbury
Brighton

Haarlem
Leyden Amsterdam
Delft   Utrecht
's Hertogenbosch
Ghent

Brunswick Berlin

Hildesheim
Corvey   Dessau

St.Riquier
Bayeux Caen
NORMANDY Rouen
Maisons
BRITTANY Poissy St.Denis
Carnac Versailles Paris
Chartres Barbizon
Fontainebleau
Chambord
Bourges Vézelay
Poitiers Dijon
St. Savin Autun

Antwerp
Bruges
Lille
Tournai Aachen
Corbie Cambrai
Amiens
Echternach
Reims
Speyer
Troyes
Isenheim
BURGUNDY
Ronchamp
Basel

Brussels Cologne
Liège
Mainz
Würzburg
Strasbourg
BAVARIA
Augsburg
Reichenau Lindau
Salzburg
St. Gall

SAXONY
Naumburg
Prague
BOHEMIA
Nuremberg
Willendorf
Melk
Munich
St. Wolfgang
Klosterneuburg
Vienna

FRANCE Kippel
Geneva
Lascaux
La Magdeleine
Santiago
de Compostela Altamira
Moissac Penne
Toulouse
Nimes
St. Gilles Arles
Avignon PROVENCE
Aix
Marseilles

AUSTRIA

LOMBARDY Cividale
Brescia
Turin Milan Verona Vicenza
Fidenza Padua Venice
Mantua
Parma
Genoa Bologna Ravenna
Prato Rimini
Pisa Florence Split
TUSCANY Arezzo
Siena Assisi
UMBRIA
Orvieto ITALY
Rome

SPAIN

Madrid
Toledo

Cordova

Granada

Barcelona

CORSICA

SARDINIA

Fossanova
Naples

APULIA

Palermo

SICILY

Oslo
Oseberg

GERMANY

SCALE OF MILES
0 50 100   200   300

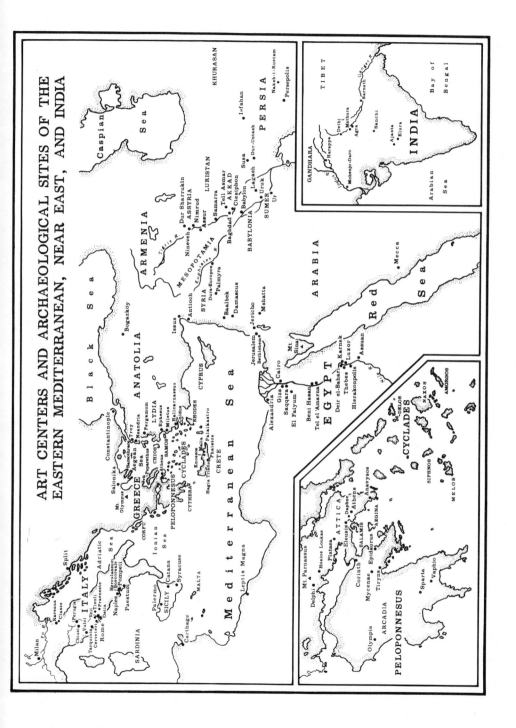

ART CENTERS AND ARCHAEOLOGICAL SITES OF THE EASTERN MEDITERRANEAN, NEAR EAST, AND INDIA